best *of* british
AIRCRAFT

Colin Higgs

bestofbritish
AIRCRAFT

First published in the UK in 2015

© Demand Media Limited 2015

www.demand-media.co.uk

Printed and bound in Europe

ISBN 978-1-910540-65-7

ABOVE
From the top...Vickers-Supermarine Spitfires Aerospatiale-BAC Concorde, Fairey Swordfish and Red Arrows BAe Systems Hawks

Contents

Chapter 1

Introduction

A successful aircraft industry needs many things...

It needs clever people, people who know what they want and are prepared to go to any length to get it. It needs co-operation, co-operation between the people designing and building aircraft and the people who will be the end users. And it needs money.

THE MEN BEHIND THE MACHINES

Since the summer of 1907 when Alliott Verdon Roe started building his first aircraft, the Roe biplane number 1, Britain's aircraft industry has been blessed with many clever people who have had quite a bit of co-operation from the money men and governments whose role is to decide what is needed and what they can afford.

Wartime is always a huge period for pace of development, meeting of minds and provision of the money needed to turn

this development potential into reality.

Consider that the first ever powered flight was in the USA in 1903 when the Wright Brothers took a short hop in their Wright Flyer and that less than fifteen years later, at the end of the First World War, many countries had committed much of their military futures to strong air forces.

In Britain it was men like Frederick Handley Page, Geoffrey de Havilland at the Royal Aircraft Factory, Tommy Sopwith, Robert Blackburn, the Short Brothers and Henry Royce at Rolls Royce who were the pioneers of the British aircraft industry and created businesses that would become household names

for decades. A positive avalanche of new aviation companies were formed in the next few years by men such as Richard Fairey and Harry Hawker while existing engineering businesses such as Vickers and Boulton & Paul rapidly diversified into aviation as well.

Some of the names are less well known. Men such as RJ Mitchell who designed the Spitfire; George Carter, who was responsible for many designs at Sopwith and Hawkers before joining Glosters and building the airframe for Britain's first jet aircraft; Sydney Camm, the designer of many great Hawker aircraft; and Roy Chadwick, chief designer at Avro.

Equally important were the men given the power over where the money was spent. These include Sir Sefton Brancker who had spent years in the Royal Flying Corps before being made Director of Civil Aviation in 1922. His enthusiasm meant that everything from local flying clubs to the building of new airports and the growth of international civil airlines was encouraged. Lord Brabazon, previously aviation pioneer Sir John Moore-Brabazon, was instrumental in shaping Britain's post-war aviation focus when a committee was formed under his name in 1942 to prepare for future civil and military aviation requirements. Lord

The Royal Flying Corps, and subsequently the Royal Air Force, grew so rapidly that when the war ended there were 22,000 aircraft on charge. In those four short years the whole concept of military flying had changed so that single and small groups of aircraft flying over the battlefield had been replaced by large formations of fighters and the new concept of strategic bombing which took the threat beyond the battlefield and into home countries, towns and cities.

Trenchard, was the first commander of Britain's newly formed independent air force, the RAF, in 1918 who fought to keep the service independent and to have the best available machines at its disposal.

MILITARY AIRCRAFT

Military aircraft building in Britain was driven by force of circumstance. Aircraft were developed for a particular role and to counter a particular threat.

In the First World War the early bombers were frail biplanes with a pilot or observer who would drop a small bomb out of the open cockpit. The V/1500, a mighty four engined bomber built by Handley Page in 1918, could fly to Berlin and drop its 2,500 lbs bomb load and fly home.

Of course between the wars the reverse was true as the government promoted peace, massively reduced spending on weaponry and dramatically reduced the RAF to almost a token force. The 'Ten Year Rule' meant that the government believed there would be no war for ten years ahead and renewed this practice every year until 1932. In that period defence spending reduced from £766 million to £102 million per annum.

However it could be said that this positively helped the RAF. The Italians bought their air force for wars in Africa during the mid 1930s. Germany developed theirs in

time for the Spanish Civil War. By the mid period of the Second World War both these air forces were being outnumbered and outgunned. The RAF had delayed its modernisation so that when it was really needed, in the Battle of Britain and for the strategic bombing offensive, theirs were the best aircraft available. And crucially the RAF had asked for, and received, aircraft that could be updated and developed. Of course these developments in aircraft were matched by the engine designers. The Rolls Royce Merlin, initially used for the Spitfire and Hurricane, was developed for many aircraft including the Lancaster bomber and Mosquito

The jet engine was the vital next step. Frank Whittle struggled for many years to get recognition and financial backing for his jet developments. In the end it was Germany that flew their jet aircraft first. Initially jet powered aircraft were actually slower than many of the more powerful piston engined ones but its development potential was huge. While the 1940s Meteor Mk.1 needed two engines because each only provided 1,700 lbs of thrust, just

15 years later the Lightning Mk.1 had two engines each producing 11,250 lbs.

In 1945 the enemy changed. The wartime RAF had been built to counter the air forces of Germany and Japan. Suddenly it was the Soviet Union that posed the threat. The Cold War was a time of huge spending again, this time on nuclear weapons, high-flying jet bombers, supersonic interceptors, missile technology and high-powered radar.

In the 1950s the British government took the aircraft industry in hand and insisted that many of the big names merged to form corporations that would be able to cope with the research, the huge cost of development and with the enormous competition from across the Atlantic. Most of the big companies disappeared into Hawker Siddeley or the British Aircraft Corporation

ABOVE
A Hawker Fury, one of the classic Hawker inter-war designs that equipped RAF squadrons in the 1930s

and any that refused, such as Sir Frederick Handley Page, were denied government patronage and soon went into liquidation.

Since then the industry has rarely built a new military aircraft in isolation. The Harrier was built with American financial assistance; Tornado was a British, German and Italian development; and the Eurofighter Typhoon is a joint venture with the construction split between companies in Britain, Germany, Italy and Spain. This is the future, the way to compete with huge US aircraft manufacturers Boeing and Lockheed Martin.

CIVIL AIRCRAFT

The growth of British civil aviation coincided with the mass availability of ex-military aircraft after the First World War. With the dismembering of the world's largest air force came dozens of new small airlines flying locally or to the continent using drafty, old wartime biplanes.

Instone Airlines was one of the first, set up in 1919, and used converted aircraft such as the DH4 to carry one or two passengers across the English Channel until merged into Imperial Airways in 1924.

In the early 1920s aircraft manufacturers regularly built small numbers of specially cre-ated aircraft for airlines. For example Bristol Aircraft built two Bristol Ten Seaters for civil use each one having a different identification as each used a different type of engine.

It was to be a few years before the manufacturers, the same ones that had built the RAF's wartime aircraft, developed special machines for civil flying.

The 1920s was the decade of development, trial and error. There were many crashes but eventually reliability improved and the 1930s became the decade of glorious air travel, visiting the Empire, carrying air mail and freight and delivering passengers round the world.

Geoffrey de Havilland led the way for Britain with the Dragon and its successor the Dragon Rapide. Handley Page built the classic HP42 and of course Short Brothers built the Empire class flying boats which were later developed into the RAF's long range Short Sunderland.

The Second World War stopped all but the most essential civil flying and even that was controlled to a large extent by the military. However after the war Britain faced the power of the enormous American aircraft building machine that had poured fighters and bombers off the production lines and then turned its focus to civil aviation.

Douglas created a stream off bestselling classics starting with the converted wartime transport, the DC-3. Lockheed built the Constellation. Boeing built the Stratocruiser and eventually moved into the 7 series staring with the 707.

Britain, though, carved a niche of its own. Avro built the York and the Tudor. De Havilland set the world alight with the first ever jet transport, the Comet. And Vickers built Britain's most successful airliner, the Viscount.

The issue was quantity. As a British manufacturer built 30 or 40, so an American one built 300 or 400 and Britain found it difficult to penetrate the American market with its huge buying potential. Vickers managed it with the Viscount and eventually BAC with the One Eleven but terrific aircraft like the Trident and VC10 never managed to make it beyond British airlines and their Empire offshoots.

The biggest mark made by British civil development, however, was Concorde, albeit in a joint venture with France. Still the only supersonic airliner to have ever entered regular service with airlines, Concorde became the best known shape in the skies for 30 years.

Now it is Airbus, the huge European consortium, where Britain places its civil expertise.

Of course the industry relies on a huge number of other businesses that have created all manner of essential elements. Martin Baker builds the world's best ejector seats. Back in the 1930s Sir Alan Cobham started a business that developed and is still the biggest in flight refuelling. Over the decades Marconi, Racal and Decca created radar and navigation systems and Irvin continue to make parachutes and survival equipment after almost 100 hundred years.

Who knows what the British Aircraft industry will be like in 20, 50 or even 100 years. The one certainty is that the great aircraft included in this book will still be talked and written about and held up as examples of how to do it right.

Chapter 2

Avro 504

Two years before the First World War started Alliott Verdon Roe received his first ever order from Britain's armed forces when they bought 12 of his E500 two-seat biplane trainers for the fledgling Royal Flying Corps.

This order gave Roe two very important things.

First he had enough money to properly establish AV Roe as a limited company and move into bigger premises.

Second it gave Roe the confidence to further develop the Avro 500 design into what would become the best training aircraft the world had seen.

Over the winter of 1912 / 1913 Roe worked on the successor to the 500 with his assistant and draughtsman, Roy

Chadwick, the man who would become famous for his designs for the Lancaster and Vulcan.

What emerged in September 1913 was an aircraft considerably in advance of anything else flying at that time. On 20 September the aircraft finished fourth in the 1913 Aerial Derby held at Hendon, a fact made all the more remarkable because it had only been flown for the first time just two days earlier.

The military showed interest in the Avro 504 immediately and placed an order for 12 aircraft which were delivered by June 1914, just two months before the outbreak of war.

What followed shows how aviation grew during the First World War. At the end of 1912 the Military Wing of the RFC had 36 aircraft and by March 1913 they had a total of 123 pilots. Just four years later at the end of the war there were over 5,000 pilots in a Royal Air Force of more than 250,000 personnel. Virtually all the pilots who flew for the RFC and RAF had been trained to fly on the Avro 504.

Some of the first 504s went to France in 1914 and took part in early bombing

OPPOSITE
The Shuttleworth Collection's Avro 504, used after the war in the film Reach for the Sky

ABOVE
The Avro Flying School's 504 trainers

operations. In 1915 an attack by Royal Naval Air Service pilots sank two U-boats near Antwerp. And on a few occasions Avro 504s were even used to intercept Zeppelins but the front line was never going to be the future for the 504.

As more orders arrived so the aircraft was consistently improved. In 1915 the first aircraft specially designed to be trainers were ordered, these being the 504A. The Navy wanted further changes and their aircraft was the 504B. But it was the decision of the commander of the new School of Special Flying at Gosport, Major Smith-Barry, which sealed the future for the 504 and the adoption of the latest variant, the J, of which 1,050 were built.

This more powerful machine allowed instructors to teach students how to recover from manoeuvres flown in aerial combat as well as the basics of flying and it led to ever bigger orders for the training units. At the end of 1917 a re-engined version became the 504K and became the standard variant for RAF training for the next ten years. In reality the 504 had been so versatile that it had kept pace with all the training needs as front line aircraft improved rapidly through the War.

By the end of the War almost 9,000 Avro 504s had been built for military requirements, more than any other wartime aircraft.

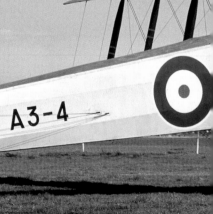

With the coming of peace thousands became available as the RAF downsized. There were many willing buyers among the general public and foreign governments and 504s became regular sights all over the world.

Avro had not finished with the aircraft though. From the start of production they had built 9,000 by the end of the war, the biggest number being the K version. Now, with the war over, Avro developed the 504N, the final major variant of which over 500 were built, bringing a total of over 10,000 Avro 504s.

Chapter 3

Sopwith Camel, Bristol F2b Fighter, SE5A

I n wartime it's vital that you stay one step ahead of the enemy and in the early months of 1917 the Royal Flying Corps was definitely behind the German Air Force in quality and effectiveness of their aircraft. However everything was about to change.

Across Britain aircraft designers had been working hard to get new improved machines ready to re-equip the front line squadrons fighting in France.

In the space of just a few months at the end of 1916 and early 1917 three new aircraft took to the skies for the first time,

three aircraft that would hugely enhance the strength of the Royal Flying Corps in its struggle for air supremacy.

The Bristol Fighter, officially the F2b, flew first in September 1916. It was a two-seater with the forward firing machine gun used by the pilot being augmented by a gunner for defence against attacks from behind. It could withstand tremendous punishment but initially the aircraft was not a success due to the outdated tactics used by pilots. By revising these tactics and treating the F2b like a single seat fighter it became hugely successful.

Second to fly was the Royal Aircraft

Factory's single-seat SE5A designed by Henry Folland and John Kenworthy at Farnborough. This was a strong and manoeuvrable aircraft which crucially was able to maintain its performance at high altitude as air combat went higher and higher as the war progressed. It was also faster than most German fighters and pilots found comfort in their ability to get away fast if outnumbered by the enemy.

The third and final one was the Sopwith Camel designed by Herbert Smith and flown for the first time by Harry Hawker in December 1916. Despite being a replacement for the viceless classic Sopwith Pup the Camel was difficult to fly in the hands of inexperienced pilots. Its powerful engine, combined with almost all the weight of the aircraft being concentrated in the first seven feet of the aircraft, would snap into a spin and killed many unsuspecting pilots. However experienced pilots used this power to their advantage, making tight rapid turns and turning the Camel into perhaps the best dogfighting aircraft of the War.

With these three classic aircraft in service from the middle of 1917 it gave the

SOPWITH CAMEL, BRISTOL F2B FIGHTER, SE5A

Royal Flying Corps a decisive advantage from which the German Air Force never recovered. During the final German offensive in the Spring of 1918 the RFC suffered heavy losses but sheer weight of numbers maintained air superiority.

As the war entered its last months Sopwith Camels, in particular, were diverted to ground attacks. This was because air combat was happening at ever greater altitude and the Camel was less effective above 12,000ft. The Spring offensive was a war of movement bringing the troops out of their trenches and into the open for the first time in years. The Camel found great success attacking the German ground forces by strafing from very low level with their machine guns and then climbing and

dropping small 25lb bombs.

Both single seat fighters, the Camel and SE5A were phased out soon after the Armistice in November 1918 as the threat of air attack disappeared. However the two-seat Bristol Fighter became a stalwart of the fledgling Royal Air Force in their post-war role of policing the British Empire. While the home-based squadrons lost their Bristol Fighters by 1920 the pilots flying over the North West Frontier in Northern India retained their aircraft until 1932 making it by far the longest serving front line aircraft introduced during the First World War.

These three aircraft deserve their reputations of being amongst the best aircraft of the War. Developed at the same time, first flown within a few months and all entering service in the Summer of 1917 they gave the RFC, and subsequently the RAF, the edge that was needed.

Consequently almost identical numbers of each one were built totalling over 16,000 aircraft, by far the largest numbers of any British front line aircraft.

De Havilland Tiger Moth

It epitomises the casual pleasure flying of the quiet pre and post-war years, warm summer days, wind in the pilot's hair, not a care in the world. There is a lot of truth in those carefree ideas but in a more difficult time the Tiger Moth was a vital part in the process of creating wartime pilots out of raw recruits.

De Havilland started their line of Moth aircraft in the late 1920s when Geoffrey de Havilland designed the DH60 Moth as a two seat touring aircraft mainly for private use and for an ever increasing number of flying clubs all over the United Kingdom. Various designs followed such as the Hawk Moth and Puss Moth before the DH82 Tiger Moth, a direct development from the Gipsy Moth, took its first flight in 1931.

The Royal Air Force required a basic trainer, an aircraft that would be easy to fly for new pupils, relatively cheap to operate and maintain but one that would introduce new pilots to aerobatics and formation flying. The Tiger Moth fitted the bill.

The Tiger Moth entered service with the RAF in 1932 and over the next few years the numbers built up until there were almost 1,000 by the outbreak of war.

Virtually all of the pilots who formed the core of the RAF's front line crews in 1939 did their initial training on a Tiger Moth. With preparations for war speeding up the numbers to be trained increased hugely and more orders were placed. To fill the gaps until more arrived many of the country's privately owned Tiger Moths were pressed into service. Wartime training of pilots is a dicey business when the country itself is in the front line

DE HAVILLAND TIGER MOTH

as the United Kingdom was at that time therefore thousands of crews were trained in Canada, South Africa and Rhodesia under the Commonwealth Air Training Plan. By the time the war ended British factories had delivered more than 4,000 Tiger Moths to the RAF. A further 2,751 were built in Australia, New Zealand and Canada bringing the total production of Tiger Moths to a staggering 8,868.

Building these aircraft was an enormous undertaking in itself. The de Havilland factories were under pressure delivering Mosquitoes so production in Britain was expanded to other companies. The Morris car factory at Cowley in

Oxford delivered more than 3,000 by the end of the war.

In 1952 the Tiger Moth began to be replaced in RAF service by the Chipmunk built by de Havilland Canada. This meant that thousands of unwanted Tiger Moths came on to the market and were snapped up by private flyers wanting a relatively cheap and easy to fly aircraft to 'potter about in'.

Internationally the aircraft was a big hit. 25 countries as diverse as Brazil and Sweden bought Tiger Moths before the war but from the late 1940s onwards Tiger Moths were used all over the world for an amazing array of jobs. In New

Zealand they were used for fertilising and crop spraying. They towed banners, dropped parachutists and pulled gliders into the air. But the main role of the Tiger Moth remained the same. Thousands of civilians took their first uncertain turn at the controls of a Tiger Moth before going on to getting a private pilot's licence.

Something like 250 Tiger Moths are still flying more than 80 years after the first flight. These gentle old aircraft still delight crowds at air shows around the world and the de Havilland Moth Club still puts on an annual Moth Rally normally in the gorgeous setting of the grounds of Woburn Abbey, a trip worth putting into the summer diary every year.

BELOW
Privately-owned Tiger Moth VH-SNT, one of many still in use round the world more than 80 years after the type was first introduced

Chapter 5

De Havilland Dragon Rapide

The de Havilland Dragon Rapide epitomises the 'golden age' of aviation, the carefree days of pre-Second World War flying when commercial aviation was still in its infancy.

De Havilland were masters at following a successful design with an even more successful one, such as the incredibly successful Moth series, and with the Dragon Rapide they enhanced their reputation enormously.

The DH84 Dragon had been designed and flown in 1932 and was a small airliner carrying up to ten passengers. De Havilland built more than 200 Dragons, more than half in the UK and the rest in Australia. The Prince of Wales flew a Dragon, as did famous record break-

ing pilot Amy Johnson, but the main customers were local British airlines like Hillmans, and Western Airways.

De Havilland's immediate successor to the Dragon was the DH86 Express, a four-engined airliner built more for longer routes and in particular for Qantas on their newly formed Empire Air Mail service route from Singapore to Australia. 62 were built and were flown all round the Empire.

However it was the DH89 Dragon Rapide that really established that classic shape in the minds of pre-war airline passengers and continues today with Rapides offering pleasure flying in many places.

The prototype Rapide first flew from Hatfield in April 1934 and the aircraft was an instant success. Hillmans Air-

ways, which had been de Havilland's first customer for the Dragon, ordered eight Rapides and that was just the beginning of a flow of orders. 25 British airlines flew the Rapide with a terrific reliability record for that time. The aircraft flew to islands around Britain's shores and connected outlying areas with main centres, some for the first time.

Compared to 21st Century airliners the Rapide was no more than a very spartan way of flying. The classic lines and beautifully designed tapering wings belied an unpressurised aircraft meaning that at heights up to 6,000 feet the passenger cabin would be extremely cold.

There was no heating, no bathroom, no lunch or drinks served and the pilot was the single crew member.

More than 200 Rapides were built for civil use in the 1930s but when war broke out in 1939 many of these were pressed into service as short haul communications and passenger aircraft. 500 new aircraft were built during the war and flown in the Royal Air Force as the de Havilland Dominie, a name that would resurface more than 20 years later as the military version of the Hawker Siddeley HS125.

Like the Tiger Moth hundreds of Dominies became surplus to requirements after the war and were snapped up

ABOVE
Forerunner of the Dragon Rapide, this DH84 Dragon was flown by Marshall Airways from Bankstown, Australia

by buyers all over the world. The instantly recognisable aircraft was soon seen plying internal routes in South America, Eastern Europe and even island hopping in the South Pacific.

Many Rapides are still flying, some of them now more than 75 years old. Pleasure flying in a classic 1930s airliner is hugely popular and you only have to see the queues at Duxford or Classic Air Force in Cornwall to see that the experience will be enjoyed for many years to come.

Blackpool and West
Coast Air Services was
one of many small
airlines that used
Dragon Rapides. Here
VIPs disembark after
their flight to Vienna

ABOVE
Dragon Rapide K4070
of 24 Squadron was
one of many Dragon
Rapides used by the
Royal Air Force for
communications flights

Chapter 6

Fairey Swordfish

RIGHT
RIGHT
An unusual view through the undercarriage of Fairey Swordfish lined up for the Fleet Review at Gosport in 1937. It shows the sturdiness needed of naval aircraft to cope with heavy landings on deck

It was a big lumbering biplane torpedo bomber. It had no right to be successful in a war when it was virtually obsolescent before the war started. But history states that the Fairey Swordfish was the most successful maritime attack aircraft employed by the allies during the Second World War. Swordfish sank more tonnage of enemy shipping than any other aircraft. And to add insult to injury its replacement, the Fairey Albacore, went out of service before the Swordfish!

At the outbreak of war the Swordfish was already an old design. It had been developed in response to a specification for a naval reconnaissance aircraft that could spot gunfire and could turn its

hand to dropping torpedoes as well. That specification had been issued in 1930. The response from Fairey was the TSRI, standing for Torpedo Spotter Reconnaissance, which crashed in September 1933. Fairey built another prototype, this time a bit more advanced, and called it the TSRII. This aircraft flew in April 1934 and orders were placed in 1935 for the Royal Navy.

The Swordfish entered service in 1936 as the main torpedo bomber in the Fleet Air Arm. 12 of the 13 naval air squadrons equipped with Swordfish in September 1939 operated off carriers such as the famous HMS Ark Royal, Glorious and Courageous but at that time there was no expectation of heroics from this aircraft.

Pilots who flew the Swordfish were the first to realise why this was to be such a successful aircraft. Solid and stable and possessing viceless handling qualities the Swordfish could cope with rolling seas and the worst weather imaginable. It had a low stalling speed and could therefore approach the deck of a carrier slowly giving the pilot time to get his landing to perfection.

During the Norwegian campaign of

FAIREY SWORDFISH

year by the Royal Navy and the only Second World War battle, the other being Trafalgar. In November 1940 the Italian fleet was in the Southern Italian harbour at Taranto threatening the allied supply lines across the Mediterranean. On one night of attacks a handful of Swordfish crippled the Italian fleet destroying or badly damaging three battleships and many smaller vessels.

The other, and perhaps more famous, attack is that of Swordfish from Ark Royal on the mighty German battleship Bismarck in May 1941. Bismarck had already sunk HMS Hood, the pride of the Royal Navy and was now making for safe waters defended by the Luftwaffe and U-boats. In a last gasp attempt to slow her down Swordfish from Ark Royal attacked and damaged Bismarck's steering giving the Royal Navy ships the chance to chase, close her down and sink her with gunfire and ship launched torpedoes.

There were many other great exploits

1940 the Swordfish scored one of its many 'firsts' when aircraft flew the first ever torpedo attack from a carrier in history. Just two days later, on 13 April 1940, a Swordfish became the first Fleet Air Arm aircraft to bomb and sink a U-boat.

It was, however, two other attacks that immortalised the Swordfish and their crew. In fact the battle of Taranto is one of only two battles celebrated every that maintained the reputation of the Fairey Swordfish but eventually, in the Spring of 1942, they were retired from their primary role. For the rest of the war Swordfish were involved in anti submarine warfare and escort duty, in particular on the MAC ships and smaller escort carriers used on the Russian convoys.

Swordfish continued in service until the end of the war before being retired in May 1945. Just one airworthy Swordfish remains, a marvellous testament to the bravery of the Swordfish crews and the amazing war record of the aircraft.

BELOW
The last flying Swordfish, LS326, of the Royal Navy Historic Flight

Bristol Blenheim

During the battle for France in May 1940 the RAF Blenheim squadrons of the Advanced Air Striking Force suffered terribly at the guns of the German fighters. Just a few months later the Blenheim night fighters were found to be more resilient in their new role but proved to be too slow to catch the even faster German bombers and were soon replaced with the speedier Beaufighters.

So it might be sensible to ask why the Blenheim should appear in a list of great British aircraft.

The Blenheim was a very important aircraft in the Royal Air Force's build up to the Second World War being the first of the modern monoplane aircraft to enter service. Over the years it was pressed into service in a variety of roles making it a true multi-role aircraft.

The evolution of the Blenheim, however, was anything but normal. In 1934 Lord Rothermere, owner of the Daily Mail, challenged the British aircraft industry to build him 'the fastest commercial aeroplane in Europe', one to challenge the fast aircraft being built in Germany and the Douglas DC-1 in the United States. Frank Barnwell, Bristol's chief designer, already had a design for a 240mph aircraft on the drawing board. Rothermere ordered what was to be called 'Britain First' and, at the same time, the Air Ministry and other air forces showed interest. 'Britain First' flew in April 1935 and immediately caused the Royal Air Force a problem. A privately-

BRISTOL BLENHEIM

BELOW
Bristol Blenheims of
141 Squadron

built aircraft, considered for military purposes as a twin-engined bomber, proved to be 50mph faster than the RAF's latest biplane fighter, the Gloster Gladiator. In August 1935 the Air Ministry ordered 150 light bomber variants and the creation of an air force that would take on Germany in 1939 was born.

By 1937 the Blenheim was in service with Bomber Command and a year later it equipped sixteen squadrons. By the outbreak of war these Mk.1s had almost all been replaced with the better Mk.IVs

and it was fifteen of these that set out on 4th September 1939 on the RAF's first bombing raid of the war.

Over the next two years Blenheims fought almost everywhere the RAF fought. After the battles for France and Britain in 1940 the RAF went on the offensive. In August 1941 Blenheim bombers flew an operation to attack a power station near Cologne, just one of the dangerous daylight raids undertaken to keep the Luftwaffe from moving all their squadrons to the Eastern front.

Although Blenheims had already been replaced by Beaufighters in Fighter Command there were four squadrons undertaking a variety of duties in Coastal Command until 1942.

Both in North Africa and flying against enemy targets in the Mediterranean the RAF kept Blenheims through to early 1943 and in the Far East they fought the Japanese until the end of that year.

Overseas the Blenheim was chosen by many air forces including Croatia, Romania and Turkey. Finland was a key partner for Bristol ordering initially in 1936 and eventually manufacturing under licence into 1941.

By the end of the war the Blenheim had completely disappeared from RAF service and as late as 1980 there was still no airworthy example flying in the world. After a twelve year restoration project a Mk.IV finally flew again in 1987 only to crash barely four weeks later. Restored again and airworthy in 1993 it flew for ten years delighting crowds at air shows all over Britain until suffering heavy damage in a landing accident at Duxford in 2003. Currently this aircraft, this time sporting a Mk. I nose, is in restoration again and is expected to fly again soon.

ABOVE
Bristol Blenheim
bombers of 44
Squadron RAF

Hawker Hurricane

Alongside the Spitfire, Lancaster and Mosquito the Hurricane is one of the four iconic British aircraft of the Second World War. However, while the other three came from new designs, new technology and new construction methods the Hurricane was the last of a great line of classic RAF fighters.

The story of the Hurricane dates from 1933 when the RAF's fighter squadrons were mainly equipped with Hawker bi-planes such as the Fury. In fact all the military air services relied heavily on Hawkers with the Fleet Air Arm using the Osprey and Nimrod, RAF bomber squadrons equipped with Hart light bombers and RAF training relying on the Hind. Therefore it seemed sensible

for the RAF to turn to Hawkers for their next front line fighter.

Through a series of designs the aircraft that finally emerged from chief designer Sydney Camm's drawing board was a streamlined monoplane using much of the well proven biplane but with retractable undercarriage, four machine guns and powered by the new Rolls Royce Merlin. A contract was placed for a prototype in February 1935 which first flew just nine months later. Within a few months Hawkers received an order for 600 Hurricanes, an unprecedented number for a peacetime air force.

111 Squadron RAF was the first to receive the new Hurricanes late in 1937, replacing its Gloster Gauntlet biplanes that had been in service for barely eighteen months and sporting an open cockpit, fixed undercarriage and a top speed of 230mph, more than 100mph slower than the Hurricane.

By September 1939, when war broke

ABOVE
The busy pre-war Hurricane production line at Hawkers in Kingston

HAWKER HURRICANE

BELOW
A Canadian-built
Hurricane Mk.X of 402
Squadron RCAF

OPPOSITE
The Last of the Many.
The final production
Hurricane being
paraded through
Kingston in 1944.
This aircraft now
flies with the BBMF

out, the RAF had nineteen squadrons equipped with Hurricanes. In total there were 497 in service with more than 3,000 still awaiting delivery. These Mark.1 aircraft had a few refinements including metal fuselage and wings, eight machine guns rather than the originally planned four and a new propellor.

Hurricanes went to France in September 1939 and were heavily involved when the Germans attacked in May 1940. Despite losses against the German Me109s this experience proved invaluable in the summer of 1940 when

Hurricanes and Spitfires flew together in the Battle of Britain.

The Battle of Britain has achieved legendary status in the annals of air warfare but it is worth taking time to recount some of the factors that show the value and abilities of the Hurricane. Hurricanes shot down 1,593 out of the 2,739 German aircraft claimed during the battle. That's 55% of the total. The Hurricane could survive much more battle damage than the Spitfire. Ease of production of the Hurricane had meant that there was never a supply problem. For this reason all the squadrons newly formed during the battle were equipped with Hurricanes. The Spitfire was undoubtedly the elegant star of the battle but the Hurricane was the cornerstone of RAF Fighter Command during that vital summer.

After the battle the Hurricane went on to prove itself as a night fighter during the Blitz of 1941. They were also used heavily in every overseas theatre of war from the hot and dusty deserts of North Africa to the steamy jungles of India and Burma. Unlike the Spitfire which was constantly developed throughout the war there were only a few further marks of Hurricane. The Mk.IIa carried a more powerful engine. The Mk.IIb was able to carry two bombs and came in to service in the spring of 1941 but perhaps the ultimate Hurricane came in 1943 with the arrival of the Mk.IV. This aircraft had a universal wing designed to carry a multitude of weaponry from 40mm cannon to rockets and bombs. It was the rocket-firing Mk.IVs which were used so effectively attacking ground targets in Burma and India.

The very last Hurricane, of 14,533, was completed in July 1944 and is now one of the few surviving aircraft flying in the world. 'The Last of the Many' is flown by the Battle of Britain Memorial Flight and is a great tribute to one of the greatest fighters of the Second World War.

Chapter 9

Vickers Wellington

The Vickers Wellington bomber was the longest serving of the three medium bombers with which RAF Bomber Command began the war. The Whitley and Hampden played valiant roles in the early bombing campaign but it was the Wellington which stood out because of its sturdy design and construction, ability to withstand substantial damage from enemy fire and huge bomb bay which meant it could carry a much bigger bomb load than either of the other two.

The Wellington was created by Rex Pierson, Vickers' chief designer, and featured a construction method designed by Barnes Wallis, perhaps best known for his bomb designs including 'Upkeep' the bouncing bomb used by the RAF to attack the great dams of Western Germany.

Wallis' geodetic design featured a spiral lattice work of metal which needed only light alloys but gave huge strength to curved surfaces. It meant that the aircraft could be badly damaged on one side but without any structural failure as the other areas would take on the load.

Development of the Wellington design took place during the early 1930s, a time of huge change in the political map of Europe. The threat imposed on the balance of power by Hitler and Mussolini made the British government speed up their search for new designs that would modernise and re-equip the armed forces.

The Wellington was built in response to a specification issued in 1932 for a

ABOVE
A Vickers Wellington of
419 Squadron RCAF

twin-engined bomber. The prototype first flew in 1936 and with a few changes to the initial design the aircraft went into production almost immediately. The Air Ministry's first order was for 180 aircraft.

99 Squadron was the first equipped with the Wellington when it went into service in October 1938 and by the outbreak of war in September 1939 there were eight fully-equipped, operational squadrons. It was Wellingtons from 9 and 149 Squadrons that mounted the

RAF's first proper bombing raid of the war on 4 September, a daylight raid against German shipping at Brunsbuttel at the mouth of the River Elbe.

It was more to do with flawed tactics that caused early losses in Wellington formations. The RAF believed that a formation of bombers without fighter support could defend itself against German opposition in daylight. Two raids in December 1939 changed their opinions as more than half of the aircraft taking part

VICKERS WELLINGTON

BELOW
During the early years of the war ground crews worked long and hard hours to keep aircraft of Bomber Command serviceable

were shot down or had to ditch in the sea.

For the next three years the Wellington played a huge part in the bomber offensive against Germany and German occupied Europe. For almost all of these raids the Wellingtons flew at night. In the 1,000 bomber raids of 1942 almost half the aircraft involved were Wellingtons and during the war the aircraft flew more than 47,000 sorties against enemy targets. They were finally withdrawn from front line night bombing operations in 1943 when ever increasing numbers of the four-engined heavy bombers were available.

Of course like any successful aircraft the Wellington was used for a variety of other roles, most noted of which were for Coastal Command either for maritime patrol or for anti-submarine operations.

A total of 11,460 Wellingtons were built and it was the only aircraft flown by the RAF to be in continuous production from before the war through until the end and beyond.

Just two complete Wellingtons survive. Of these the most famous is N2980 which was raised from the bed of Loch Ness in 1985 and restored. It is now on view at the Brooklands Museum in Weybridge in Surrey where it was originally built in 1939 - a fitting testimony to all the Wellington crewmen who flew and fought in the Second World War.

LEFT
An advertisement for the latest role of the Wellington. The huge magnetic ring was used by low flying aircraft to detect and blow up floating mines

BELOW
A Wellington Mk.XIII painted white and used by RAF Coastal Command

Supermarine Spitfire

The Spitfire is perhaps the most famous aircraft in British aviation history.

Its wartime record coupled with the classic shape of its elliptical wings and the instantly recognisable sound of its Merlin engine make it one of the most popular aircraft at air shows almost 75 years after its finest hour during the Battle of Britain in 1940.

The Spitfire was the brainchild of RJ Mitchell, the chief designer at Vickers Supermarine,

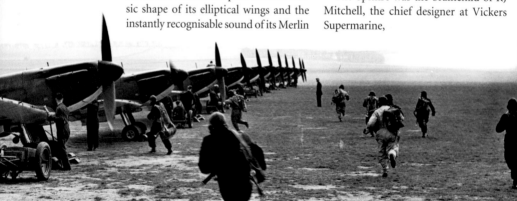

who had also been responsible for a series of successful, record-breaking racing seaplanes. The S.5, S.6 and S.6B had claimed the Schneider Trophy outright by winning three races in a row between 1927 and 1931. And while there are no common features between them and the Spitfire there is no doubt that his success inspired him to develop the greatest piston-engined fighter ever.

The secret of the Spitfire's success lay in the design together with the Air Ministry's agreement to finance it and the arrival of the great Rolls Royce Merlin engine all coupled with Mitchell's ability to put it all together in such a spectacular package.

The prototype Spitfire, K5054, flew for the first time at Eastleigh in Hampshire on 5 March 1936. Within four months it had flown in public at the Hendon Air Pageant and the Air Ministry had placed their first order. Sadly Mitchell died from cancer in June 1937 but his work on the development of the Spitfire was continued by Joe Smith, Mitchell's chief draughtsman.

The first order was for 310 aircraft but it was obvious the RAF would want plenty more. Despite the creation of the first Spitfire production line in Southampton plans went ahead for a huge new Spitfire factory at Castle Bromwich in the West Midlands.

ABOVE
Some of the surviving Battle of Britain Spitfire pilots at the 60th anniversary celebrations for the Spitfire in 1996 at Duxford

SUPERMARINE SPITFIRE

The RAF's first Spitfire squadron, number 19, took delivery of its aircraft during the summer of 1938. There were ten Spitfire squadrons by the outbreak of war and 19 by the start of the Battle of Britain.

No Spitfires went to France in 1939 and none were involved in the early fighting after the German attacks on 10 May 1940. However the Spitfires saw their first combat towards the end of May and intensively over the beaches of Dunkirk.

Throughout the Battle of Britain in the summer of 1940 Hurricanes and Spitfires flew in defence of the country. There were a lot more Hurricanes and they shot down more aircraft but it was the classic Spitfire that epitomised Britain's dogged defence. This was helped by the creation of Spitfire funds whereby local communities would club together to raise the £5,000 needed to build a Spitfire.

After the Battle of Britain the Spitfire got better and better. The Mark V dominated Fighter Command squadrons in Europe when it came into service in 1941 until the even more advanced Mark IX came in a year later and became the standard variant until the end of the War.

In 1942 Supermarine started fitting the bigger and much more powerful supercharged Rolls Royce Griffon engine into some new Spitfires. This meant a change of design and parts of the classic Spitfire shape disappeared. 1,836 Griffon-engined Spitfires were produced across six variants among which was the

final Spitfire, the Mark.24.

During the war Spitfires flew successfully in every theatre of war. This showed the benefit of the modern design that Mitchell had created and the way it was able to be developed constantly including for the Royal Navy as a fleet fighter called the Seafire.

In all the production of Spitfires totalled almost 22,000 of which over 2,000 were Seafires. Despite all the development and new engines by far the largest number were of the Merlin-powered Mark.V.

The Spitfire remains a classic. Packed with power, but both graceful and elegant, it's no wonder that they thrill crowds at air shows all over the World.

Chapter 11

Short Sunderland

Short Brothers of Belfast had an enviable reputation for the design and manufacture of flying boats from the early years of military aviation before the First World War into the 1930s. Short Singapores, Rangoons and many others were mainstays of the RAF's flying boat squadrons both in home waters and around the Empire.

Undoubtedly the best of them was the Sunderland, an enormous four-engined beast with a crew of 13, which went into service with the Royal Air Force in 1938 and stayed on front-line duties for 20 years. It was developed as a military version of the Imperial Airways 'C' class Empire flying boats of the 1930s that did so much to promote civil air travel before the Second World War.

The Sunderland was instantly recognisable with its very deep hull and high wings to keep the propellors away from

BELOW
Sunderlands waiting
at the docks for their
delivery flights to RAF
Squadrons

SHORT SUNDERLAND

BELOW
The final production
Sunderland awaiting
departure in June 1946

OPPOSITE
One of the RNZAF
Sunderlands
undergoing extensive
maintenance

the sea. It was a real boat and it came on shore very rarely, spending most of its time moored to a buoy when not on active service.

The Sunderland became one of the most versatile aircraft in the RAF's Coastal Command. It was used for many duties including long range reconnaissance, anti-submarine patrols, convoy protection, long distance transportation and air sea rescue. It had a formidable defensive armament of twelve machine guns and many an enemy fighter pilot, believing this big aircraft would be easy prey, was driven off by the guns of a Sunderland gaining it the nickname 'the flying porcupine' from the Germans. Offensively the Sunderland could carry up to 5,000 lbs of bombs, depth charges or mines.

One of the most important aspects of the Sunderland's performance was its endurance. Crews regularly flew patrols lasting more than thirteen hours and flying more than 2,500 miles. This meant that huge areas of ocean could be kept safe from enemy activity.

Sunderlands were active across the world during the war. They flew convoy patrols over the South Atlantic; they hunted U-boats in the North Atlantic, sinking 27 from 1940 to 1944, and Japanese submarines in the Indian Ocean; they pulled stranded sailors from the water in the North Sea and evacuated British troops from Crete and Norway. Seemingly there was nowhere a Sunderland would not go.

After the war, despite an increasing reliance on long range landplanes for maritime duties, the Sunderlands continued to provide magnificent service. They flew throughout the Korean War and carried almost five thousand tons of supplies into Lake Havel in Berlin during the humanitarian airlift in 1948. In particular they were very useful for carrying salt. In normal land planes salt would rapidly corrode the metal in the fuselage but being flying boats they were already protected against corrosion from seawater so no further damage could come to them.

It was not until May 1959 when the last remaining RAF Sunderlands, based at Seletar in Singapore, flew on active service for the last time, thereby ending the RAF's long love affair with flying boats. However the Royal New Zealand Air Force continued with Sunderlands until 1967, almost exactly 30 years after the aircraft's first flight.

Sunderlands were also adapted for civilian use. BOAC, Qantas and other airlines operated them from 1942 onwards carrying passengers and mail across the Empire.

749 Sunderlands were built at factories in Rochester in Kent and Belfast but sadly there are very few left and only one of those is now airworthy.

Chapter 12

Handley Page Halifax

While there is no doubt that the Avro Lancaster was the most successful British heavy bomber of the Second World War the Halifax ran it a close second.

Arriving earlier than the Lancaster and equipping squadrons with a huge variety of versions to suit a wide range of tasks the Halifax earns a place in any list of great British aircraft and its story should not need to be compared with that of its illustrious partner.

The Halifax first flew just a few weeks after the outbreak of war in 1939 and began to equip RAF Bomber Command squadrons in November 1940. Its first operation was an attack on Le Havre on 11 March 1941 when six aircraft from 35

Squadron bombed naval targets. It also became the first RAF heavy bomber to drop bombs on German targets when attacking Hamburg the following night of 12 March 1941. After many years of development, and the disappointment of the introduction of the Short Stirling into Bomber Command earlier in 1941, the Royal Air Force finally had an effective heavy bomber to lead the attacks on Hitler's Germany.

Over the next year there were many modifications to the Halifax needed mainly because of a lack of speed. There were also problems with the aircraft's bomb carrying abilities as the bomb bay could not carry the 4,000lb 'Cookie' bomb which was "Bomber" Harris' preferred weapon of destruc-

HANDLEY PAGE HALIFAX

tion against German cities. While the issues with the bomb bay were never properly fixed the performance of later versions of the Halifax improved enormously. The Mk.III, which appeared in service from February 1944, finally gave the aircraft the performance required. Restrictions stopping the Halifax attacking more hazardous targets were lifted and it was now able to take

a full part in the bombing offensive.

At its peak in 1944 Halifaxes equipped twenty six RAF bomber squadrons almost all in 4 Group and 6 Group, based at airfields in Yorkshire, with many of them crewed by Canadians.

By this time the Halifax had found many other roles. In Coastal Command it was used for anti submarine warfare and general reconnaissance. They were

also used for special operations such as dropping SOE agents into enemy occupied territory or dropping the SAS behind enemy lines in France. They towed gliders and carried electronic jamming equipment to confuse German night fighters. In fact there was very little the Halifax could not do.

Of course the main role of the Halifax was as a heavy night bomber and during the war it flew 75,532 sorties and dropped a million tons of bombs on enemy targets.

6,176 Halifaxes were built from 1939 until the last one rolled off the production line in April 1945. They continued in service with the RAF until 1952 but many converted bombers were used after the war as transport aircraft. In fact many were used to move supplies into Berlin during the airlift in 1949.

Many years after the war there are still plenty of bomber crewmen alive to tell their stories. Of these the Halifax crews will tell you how the Mk.III Halifax was actually a better aircraft and better bomber than the Lancaster used at the same time. Whatever is the truth there is no doubt that the Halifax was a great bomber for the RAF.

Chapter 13

De Havilland Mosquito

BELOW
Final checks on the reassembled Mosquito prototype at Hatfield before its first flight in November 1940

In the age of metal fuselages and wings how could an aircraft largely built of wood possibly become one of the most famous British aircraft ever and arguably the best British military aircraft of the Second World War?

The Mosquito was built by the de Havilland Aircraft Company which had already created classics such as the Tiger Moth and Dragon Rapide. It would prove to be the most versatile aircraft in the Royal Air Force's wartime inventory being used as bomber, day and night fighter, for reconnaissance, pathfinding, minelaying and photographic roles as well as in Coastal Command for attacks on enemy shipping. It could patrol, intrude, attack and evade as well as anything else flying at the time.

It was Bomber Command's fastest aircraft of the war and would stay the fastest

DE HAVILLAND MOSQUITO

DE HAVILLAND MOSQUITO

until the introduction of the jet powered Canberra in 1951.

Origins of the Mosquito date back to a 1936 Air Ministry specification for a twin-engined bomber capable of carrying 3,000lbs of bombs. It was Geoffrey de Havilland, however, who suggested that this bomber could be made of wood as it was assumed that the metal required would be in short supply. He also had experience of building modern wooden aircraft with the de Havilland Albatross airliner. He teamed this experience with the availability of the great Rolls Royce Merlin engine and created a classic, clean design that became a world-beater.

It was not until December 1939 that de Havilland were given the go-ahead by the Air Ministry to proceed with the design. Many changes and additions were requested but the prototype that first flew on 25 November 1940 was remarkably virtually unaltered from Geoffrey de Havilland's initial vision, a twin-engined light bomber with two crew that was so fast that it needed no defensive armament.

The first production aircraft were supposed to be for 50 bombers but the importance of the Battle of Britain led to the Air Ministry altering the initial Mosquito order to 20 bombers and 30 fighters. By the end of its amazing pro-

duction run of almost 7,800 aircraft less than 25% were bombers.

The mosquitoes exploits from the time it first went into action in May 1942 until the end of the War are legendary but perhaps just one set of attacks sum up the aircraft. From February 1945 for 36 successive nights Mosquitos attacked Berlin, the German capital. They flew at heights up to 40,000 feet and the force only lost .05% of the aircraft involved. That's just one aircraft for every 2,000 that attacked. More than 2,500 sorties were flown by Bomber Command's Light Night Striking Force of Mosquitoes over those 36 nights and they continued to attack major German targets through to the end of the war.

After the war Mosquitoes equipped RAF squadrons until 1953 when the last of the type were withdrawn. However that classic shape was not lost to Britain's skies for a few years to come. De Havilland had privately developed a long range single seat aircraft which was a completely new design but included much of the classic Mosquito as well. The Hornet first flew in 1944 and started to equip RAF squadrons from 1946. The Hornet was best known for its active service in Malaya where they flew thousands of attacks against Communist guerillas. There was even a naval version, the Sea Hornet, which equipped Fleet Air Arm squadrons from 1949.

Avro Lancaster

By 1942 the allied bombing offensive against Germany was faltering. The twin engined front-line bombers used since the beginning of the war, such as Whitleys and Hampdens, had outlived their usefulness. They couldn't fly high or fast enough and their bomb-carrying capacity was woefully low. They also couldn't survive against ever-improving enemy fighters. Among these bombers was the Avro Manchester, an aircraft that had great potential but constantly suffered with engine problems. Instead of developing this aircraft the Air Ministry decided to put its support behind a new version.

As a direct result of the failure of the Manchester came a four-engined version

fitted with Rolls Royce Merlin engines which flew for the first time in January 1941. From that prototype very few changes were made before the Royal Air Force began to receive the aircraft, renamed the Lancaster, in great numbers.

44 Squadron, based at Waddington in Lincolnshire, was the first RAF squadron to receive Lancasters. They flew them on a few mining operations before the first proper bombing operation. On 17 April 1942 six Lancasters from each of 44 and 97 Squadrons attacked a diesel factory near Augsburg in Germany. It was a low-level daylight raid and seven aircraft were shot down. Much damage was inflicted on the factory and the mission leader, John Nettleton, was awarded the Victo-

ria Cross. This was just the first of many spectacular raids on which the Lancaster would create a legend.

The history of the Lancaster in RAF Bomber Command is one of continuous success. They were chosen for virtually every major bombing operation for the rest of the war. Perhaps most famous of all was the 'Dambusters' raid carried out on the night of 16 May 1943. 617 Squadron was formed specially for the operation, one that had a massive impact on the morale of Bomber Command, the RAF and the whole country. It created heroes in the leader Guy Gibson who was awarded a Victoria Cross and Barnes

BELOW
The Lancaster prototype BT308 seen at Avro's factory at Woodford after completing its first flight at Ringway airport in Manchester on 9 January 1941

AVRO LANCASTER

Wallis the brilliant designer of the bouncing bomb that breached the Mohne and Eder Dams.

617 became the squadron of choice when a difficult operation was scheduled. Every time the Lancaster was called on to perform with bigger and bigger bombs a little modification made it possible. In November 1944 the squadron sunk the German battleship Tirpitz in a Norwegian fjord using 12,000 lbs 'Tallboy' bombs. By the end of the war 617 Squadron Lancasters carried 22,000 lbs 'Grand Slam' bombs into Germany and destroyed vital targets with accurate bombing.

Lancasters formed the backbone of the newly formed Pathfinder Force from 1942 and at the end of the war they were used in numbers to drop food to the starving Dutch population in Operation

Lancasters continued in service with the RAF until 1956 but mainly with Coastal Command as the bombers were replaced by new Lincolns coming off the Avro production line.

Now there are two remaining airworthy Lancasters, one in Canada and perhaps the most famous of them all, PA474, flown by the Battle of Britain Memorial Flight as a tribute to the 55,000 men of Bomber Command killed during the Second World War.

Manna. In March 1945, just a few weeks from the end of the war, Bomber Command had 745 Lancasters in 56 front line squadrons. When hostilities ceased many of these aircraft were used to repatriate many of the 75,000 allied prsioners of war liberated from German POW camps.

The statistics for the Lancaster are amazing. 7,377 were built between 1941 and the end of 1945. They flew 156,000 sorties during the war, dropping more than 608,000 tons of bombs and an incredible 51 million incendiaries. Being at the forefront of the action Lancasters bore the brunt of heavy bomner losses with 3,249 being lost in action and 21,000 crewmen killed.

Hawker Typhoon

The Hawker Typhoon had a troubled start to life and it was a few years before it finally found its role. From that time it became one of the most formidable weapons in the RAF's wartime armoury.

As early as 1937, when the Kingston factory was finishing construction of the first batch of Hurricanes, Hawkers were already looking at a successor. Sydney Camm designed a 12-gun fighter with bigger engines and therefore more speed, pre-empting what the Air Ministry might need.

The Typhoon flew for the first time in February 1940 but, partly due to early testing problems and partly due to a need to increase the production on the Hurricane, the Typhoon's development was delayed. There was a problem with the wing; it was too thick which meant too much drag at speeds above 400mph. There were dif-

HAWKER TYPHOON

ferent guns fitted in different prototypes. However such importance had been attached to the Typhoon that it was rushed into service with Fighter Command in 1941 to combat the FW190 which was outclassing the Spitfire Mk.V.

The Typhoon was not up to the job. Its rate of climb was too slow. Too many accidents occurred. Exhaust fumes were leaking into the cockpit and despite these issues being fixed the aircraft had got itself a bad name with pilots. Its days as an interceptor were numbered.

However the commander of 609 Squadron, the then Squadron Leader Ro-

land Beamont, suggested that rather than scrap the Typhoon it should be used for ground attack instead. All the focus had been put on the aircraft's issues at height while seemingly ignoring its qualities at low level.

From the end of 1942, after more than a year of service with the RAF, the Typhoon finally found its role. Rather than try to defend Britain's skies against superior German fighters Typhoons became potent offensive weapons in support of ground forces.

Typhoons were converted to carry a variety of bombs but it was the provision of rockets that made it so effective. Towards the end of 1943 Typhoons proved their worth by attacking enemy shipping to great effect and 18 Squadrons were attached to the newly formed 2TAF, or Second Tactical Air Force, in the lead up to the D-Day landings in Normandy.

Marauding Typhoons attacked almost anything that moved. Troops, gun emplacements, railways, radar installations, ammunition dumps and road convoys were all attacked and destroyed in the weeks before D-Day rendering German forces almost incapable of sustained movement.

After the landings on 6 June 1944

Typhoons flew in close support of the ground forces as they developed a 'cab rank' system whereby ground commanders could call in aircraft to attack enemy forces directly affecting their advance through Normandy. Perhaps the Typhoons' finest hour was at Falaise. In July the retreating German forces found themselves squeezed between the advancing American forces from the south and the British from the north. Constantly harried by Typhoon attacks the German commanders had no option than to abandon their vehicles on the congested roads and get away as quickly as possible. Even though claims of huge numbers of enemy tanks destroyed proved to be massively over inflated the sheer terror wreaked on the German forces was tremendous. Firing their rockets in the first pass the Typhoons would attack again and again using their 20mm cannon, strafing the stationary vehicles and causing chaos.

Typhoon support continued right to the end of the war but as soon as it was over they started disappearing from the RAF. Disbanded altogether or replaced with the new Tempest Mk. V the Typhoon's contribution had been essential but its time was up.

BELOW
A Typhoon 1b of 197 Squadron in 1944. As a fighter bomber it became one of the most devastating weapons in the RAF's arsenal

Chapter 16

Gloster Meteor

BELOW
The Gloster E28-39, the
research aircraft built
to test Britain's first jet
engine, the Whittle W.1

George Carter had a great career in aviation. He worked at Hawkers, Sopwith, de Havilland and Short Bros before joining Gloster in 1931. He was still only 42 and had built up a wealth of experience in aircraft design. At Gloster he worked with chief designer Henry Folland on the Gauntlet and Gladiator, two classic biplanes that served the RAF with distinction in the late 1930s.

In April 1939 Carter met Frank Whittle, an RAF officer who had spent many years developing a gas turbine engine. Carter was present when Whittle's engine was successfully bench-tested and it was from these meetings that the two worked together on what would become Britain's first jet aircraft, the Gloster Meteor.

The Meteor development began as the Gloster E28/39, a specification issued by the Air Ministry in February 1940 for a single-engined small research aircraft to be powered by Whittle's W.1 gas turbine engine.

Flying for the first time in May 1941 trials with the E28/39 were very successful and led to the development of a twin-engined aircraft.

These early Whittle engines had very little power and it was Carter's view that two would be needed to make any feasible fighter aircraft. Mock ups were created even before the E28/39 had flown and within a few months both prototypes and an initial production order of 250 had been placed for this revolutionary aircraft.

The first Meteor prototype flew on 5 March 1943 with subsequent proto-types all flying with different engines as the designers tried to find out the best configuration. Eventually Rolls Royce took on the engine manufacture and the Meteor that would enter service with the RAF was born.

In July 1944 the first production Meteor was delivered to the first RAF squadron, 616 based at Culmhead in Somerset where they tested the new aircraft before moving to Manston in Kent from where operations began almost immediately.

On 4 August a 616 Squadron Meteor flown by Fg. Off. 'Dixie' Dean destroyed a V1 flying bomb, the first victory for a British jet fighter. However it was not a

GLOSTER METEOR

'normal' kill for a fighter pilot. Despite his cannon jamming he had enough speed from his jet engine to catch up with the V1, tip its wing over with his own and the V1 crashed to the ground.

More success followed and their aircraft were replaced by Mark 3s in January 1945. That same month they were deployed to Europe for the first time but forbidden to fly into enemy occupied territory in case one was shot down and captured by Germans.

By June 1945, and with the war in Europe won, the first Meteor wing was formed at Colerne in Wiltshire. There were three squadrons, 616 being augmented by 504 and 74 Squadrons.

In 1946 a further step change in performance was provided by the Mark 4 which had much more powerful engines and increased speed by over 150 mph. That same year RAF Fighter Command pledged itself to an all jet future when the de Havilland Vampire was introduced alongside the Meteor. The Mark 8 became the final fighter variant and equipped 30 RAF squadrons until phased out in 1957.

Meteor fighters were replaced by Hawker Hunters but they found new variants performed very well in ground attack, reconnaissance and night fighting roles until the type was finally withdrawn from service in 1961.

Internationally the Meteor made a big impact. The Royal Australian Air Force operated Meteors in Korea and both Egypt and Israel used them during the Suez crisis in 1956. In Europe France, Belgium, West Germany and the Netherlands all operated Meteors.

Almost 4,000 were built of Britain's first ever jet fighter, the aircraft on which the RAF built its jet future.

BELOW
'The Meteorites'. A team of four Meteor T7s from CFS in 1952 and 53 became the first ever RAF team to have a name

Chapter 17

De Havilland Vampire

W hile the Gloster Meteor took all the plaudits for being Britain's first jet aircraft the de Havilland Vampire had many 'firsts' of its own during its more than 20 year history with the RAF.

In the same way that there had been a fortuitous meeting between George Carter and Frank Whittle, Geoffrey de Havilland was approached to design an airframe to fit the experimental jet engine designed by Frank Halford.

Halford had been a car racer and engine designer for many years. His most famous engine had been the Napier Sabre which powered aircraft such as the Typhoon and Tempest but this had a relatively short life with the introduction of jet technology. Now his first jet engine, the H1, was developed and built by de Havilland as the Goblin 1.

What de Havilland created was a decidedly experimental design. It was a small, twin-boom, straight winged, single-engined jet fighter armed with cannon. The Air Ministry issued a specification to the de Havilland design in 1942 and the prototype first flew barely 16 months later.

Orders placed in May 1944 meant that the Vampire would be too late to take part in the Second World War but became the RAF's second jet-powered fighter when it entered service in 1946. This was the first time the RAF had an aircraft that could fly faster than 500mph.

Vampires became part of the Second Tactical Air Force in Germany and also equipped squadrons in the newly formed Vampire Wing at RAF Odiham in Hampshire. 247 Squadron was the first to receive them in April 1946 and it was their pilots who flew in the Victory Flypast over London in June of that year. They flew Vampires for five years, successively equipped

OPPOSITE
A Vampire FB.9 of 20 Squadron RAF based at Oldenburg in Germany

ABOVE
Vampire FB.5 VV217 which was used extensively for flight testing at de Havilland Hatfield

RIGHT
Formation of four
Vampire T.11 trainers
from 5FTS based
at Oakington near
Cambridge

with the Mk.1, Mk.3 and eventually the FB.5, the aircraft that became the standard Vampire of Fighter Command.

The Vampire was also the first jet fighter to equip Royal Auxiliary Air Force squadrons when 605 replaced its Mosquito night fighters.

For the next few years Vampires were used on many record attempts, experimental tests and overseas sales trips.

In April 1948 six Vampires from 54 Squadron made the first ever jet crossing of the Atlantic. Led by Battle of Britain ace, Bobby Oxspring, they subsequently toured Canada and the United States. De Havilland test pilot John Cunningham set a new altitude record in an adapted aircraft when he flew to 59,446 feet. Other aircraft were fitted with experimental engines including the Rolls Royce Nene which would go on to power two naval aircraft, the Attacker and the Sea Hawk. The Royal Navy showed an early interest and famous pilot, Captain Eric 'Winkle' Brown became the first man to land a jet fighter on board an aircraft carrier in December 1945. This led to orders for a navalised version to be built. The Sea Vampire went into service in late 1948 and became the Royal Navy's first jet aircraft.

DE HAVILLAND VAMPIRE

32 countries bought Vampires including the Swiss Air Force, which began a trend of flying British-built aircraft, Egypt and Canada. In many cases these countries followed their purchase of singe-seaters with orders for the new two-seat Vampire trainers which first flew in 1950.

The Vampire trainer was a logical move after the introduction of the fighter.

The RAF needed an advanced jet trainer with bigger and more complicated jet fighters due in service. Aircraft such as the Hunter would be hard to master with no equivalent trainer. By the mid 1950s students found it much better to move from Jet Provost through the Vampire and onto their eventual front line fighter.

3,268 Vampires were built before production ended in 1958.

Chapter 18

Avro Shackleton

A nother great workhorse from the drawing board at Avro, the splendid and versatile Shackleton filled a vital role for the Royal Air Force for forty years making it one of Britain's longest serving aircraft.

At the end of the Second World War the lend-lease aircraft that had arrived in their thousands from the United States started to leave Britain and return across the Atlantic. Among them were the Fortresses and Liberators that had provided much of the long range maritime patrol role for Britain's lifelines abroad. It was this gap in the RAF's armoury that the Shackleton was destined to fill.

Originating from the classic Lancaster bomber Avro's designer Roy Chadwick had built both the Lincoln bomber and the Tudor airliner. It was from these two aircraft that the Shackleton was derived. The aircraft was named after determined polar adventurer, Sir Ernest Shackleton, but it was Chadwick who chose the name as his wife was descended from the explorer.

The prototype of the Shackleton was flown by Avro chief test pilot Jimmy Orrell on 9 March 1949. It could carry bombs, depth charges or torpedoes and was fitted with machine guns. It had a crew of 10 and was powered by four Rolls Royce Griffon engines.

The second prototype had lost many of the unnecessary elements and was much more like the eventual production aircraft that went into service with 120 Squadron RAF at Kinloss in Scotland in 1951.

ABOVE
Avro Shackleton GR1
VP256 based at RAF
Ballykelly in Northern
Ireland

So began the creation of a legend in the RAF. Men who became part of a Shackleton crew tended to stay as 'Shackleton Men' for the rest of their careers and beyond. Regular 15 hour patrols over endless seas with the constant growling of the engines tended to either drive people out rapidly or gain a similar sense of endurance to that of the aircraft. The life of a Shackleton crew, however, did include a few diverse operations and a bit of variety. On occasions they were used for troop carrying. In 1956, during the Suez crisis, Shackletons were used for anti-submarine duties for the first time, security for the British and French ships moored off the Egyptian coast. They were used for disaster relief and even recreated the old goodwill visits undertaken by the RAF's flying boats in the 1920s and 30s.

ABOVE
Now converted to MR1
standard VP256 flying
with 269 Squadron RAF

The main duties for the Shackletons in the early years, however, were search and rescue and those long hours patrolling the sea lanes from their bases in South West England, Northern Ireland, Gibraltar and Malta.

In 1954 the last of the RAF's Sunderland flying boats were withdrawn from service so there was a need for the Shackletons to take on even longer patrols. The new MR3 variant could stay airborne for up to 24 hours and 18 hours became a regular operation duration.

Later still, in 1967, the Shackleton took on its final role, that of airborne early warning. 12 older MR2s were converted and formed 8 Squadron at Kinloss in 1972. That same year the remaining Shackletons were withdrawn and replaced by the Nimrod leaving the 8 Squadron aircraft in their new role to continue the Shackleton tradition of coping admirably with every role thrown at it.

The only overseas destination for Shackletons was South Africa which pur-chased eight MR3s. They were operated by the South African Air Force from 1957 until 1984.

Out of the 185 built three potential airworthy Shackletons have survived with many others on static display in muse-ums round the world. None currently fly but it is hoped that this great aircraft will grace the skies again in the future.

BELOW
The Avro Shackleton
MR.3 prototype in
1955, the year before
it crashed

Chapter 19

English Electric Canberra

The English Electric Canberra is probably the most versatile and definitely the longest serving aircraft ever in the RAF's history. It was designed to replace the bomber version of the Mosquito after the Second World War but ended up taking on a bewildering range of roles from high and low level conventional bomber, strategic nuclear bomber, trainer for many different armed services and photo reconnaissance to night intruder, electronic counter measures and were even used as remote controlled drones for target towing.

Developed in the last months of the war by English Electric from a design by Teddy Petter the Canberra, then simply

known as the A1, first flew in May 1949. At the controls was Roland Beamont who would later test fly the Lightning and the TSR2. The simple design teamed with two powerful jet engines meant that the Canberra rapidly came to the attention of many air forces around the world. It could fly very high, higher in fact than most fighters, and very fast. Beamont himself told a story of the first time he flew the Canberra to the United States. Unaware that an aircraft could fly that fast and that high the American authorities put New York on alert for flying saucers!

Almost unprecedented in peacetime the Canberra entered service with the RAF less than two years after its first flight. The ultimate bomber version for the RAF, the B.6, first went to war

in 1955 when 101 Squadron was sent to Malaya and was used against terrorists in the Malayan jungle. Less than two years later Canberras were operating during the Suez crisis. Based in Cyprus 88 aircraft were deployed attacking Egyptian military targets. By this time Canberras equipped 27 squadrons of the Royal Air Force and constituted the mainstay of Bomber Command. However the growing importance of the strategic nuclear deterrent saw the rapid build up of the V-force during the late 1950s and these new aircraft, the Vulcan, Victor and Valiant, provided the long range, high payload capabilities that the Canberra could not match. By 1961 Canberra bombers had been retired from Bomber

Command followed a few years later by those deployed overseas.

But the service life of the Canberra was barely just beginning. Photo reconnaissance variants entered service in 1952 with the last ones, the PR9s of 39 Squadron at Marham, not retiring until 2006, a staggering 54 years later. And at the end of their service these venerable old aircraft were still flying vital missions over Afghanistan.

As late as 1987 new versions were still entering service with the T17A equipping 360 Squadron in an electronic counter measures jamming enemy radar.

The huge success of the aircraft in the RAF interested many air forces internationally. 16 other countries eventually operated Canberras from African countries such as Ethiopia and Rhodesia to South American countries such as Venezuela and Argentina. However perhaps the most important partner was the United States who, looking for a suitable light tactical bomber and reconnaissance aircraft, chose to build under license the Canberra as the Martin B-57. More than 400 B-57s were built including a number for Pakistan and China.

Including the B-57s more than 1,400 aircraft were built making it one of the most numerous of peacetime aircraft. And now that the Canberra is almost a pensioner there are still flying examples delighting air show crowds in different parts of the world.

BELOW
The Canberra's 40th anniversary was celebrated in 1989 with this line up of TT.18s from 100 Squadron at RAF Wyton

Chapter 20

De Havilland Comet

Less than four years after the end of the Second World War the de Havilland Comet became the first commercial jetliner to fly, a remarkable journey from Frank Whittle's pre-war and wartime experiments with jet propulsion.

Based on Brabazon Committee recommendations the Ministry of Supply issued a contract to de Havilland for what was called the Type 106 in February 1945. After various modifications to the original specification the aircraft that first flew in July 1949 was an all-metal, 36 seat airliner powered by four jet engines.

It must have been a dream for the de Havilland design and testing team as the new aircraft, named the Comet, passed trouble free testing with flying colours. The primary operator BOAC was happy with their own testing and the aircraft went into production with the first 10

Comet 1s being delivered through the summer of 1952. Overseas orders flooded in as BOAC halved their previous flying times to destinations such as Tokyo and South Africa.

Even as the first aircraft were being delivered one or two 'incidents' started to place doubt in people's minds. Two of them were blamed on pilot error while a third, which killed all forty three

undertaken. The outcome was metal fatigue. Prolonged changes in pressure had resulted in cracks at the weakest points, the corners of square windows. The windows were changed and the fuselages strengthened. De Havilland developed the Comet 2 and subsequently the Comet 4 which became the most successful mark of Comet ever built.

The Comet 4 was used by BOAC to open up the first ever transatlantic jetliner route to the United States in October 1958. Over the next few months Comets took over the routes to the Caribbean, Ceylon, Australia, Japan, South Africa and many other countries. The 19 Comet 4s of BOAC flew an astonishing 27,000,000 miles in their first two years of operation.

This new, safe and successful aircraft regained many of the sales lost when the Comet 1 crashes grounded the fleet. Argentina was the first country to order followed rapidly by Capital Airlines from the USA, Mexico, Greece and the Middle East. British airlines Dan-Air and BEA also flew Comets on their European services.

In 1961 de Havilland received its first orders for the Comet 4 from Britain's Royal Air Force beginning a relationship with the aircraft that would last 50 years.

passengers and crew, was put down to a severe storm. The aircraft crashed just a few miles from the airport at Calcutta in India with eyewitnesses reporting they had seen a wingless airliner diving into the sea.

Within a few months of each other early in 1954 two further BOAC Comets crashed soon after take off, both from Rome and both with the loss of everyone on board. All Comets were grounded. So began one of the longest and most thorough accident investigations ever

These first five aircraft for Transport Command carried troops and their families across the world as well as ambulance duties carrying wounded servicemen back to the UK until 1975.

Although not strictly a Comet the RAF's successful maritime patrol aircraft, the Hawker Siddeley Nimrod, was an extensively modified Comet. The first of 49 aircraft entered service in 1969 and became a vital part of the RAF's defensive capabilities until 2010.

Those initial problems perhaps stopped the Comet becoming a world-wide success but there is no doubt that the Comet 4 was a safe and successful airliner and a worthy successor to the world's first commercial jet airliner.

LEFT
Test pilot John Cunningham (centre) with Comet C.2 XK716 at Broughton in May 1957

BELOW
A Comet 4c of Dan-Air. By this time the Comet's role had changed dramatically from luxurious first-class airliner to package tour stalwart

Chapter 21

Vickers Viscount

The Vickers Viscount is a true classic, a milestone in civil aviation and the most successful British airliner ever built.

It was the first gas turbine engined aircraft to carry passengers. The Rolls Royce Dart engines were so hugely reliable that the Viscount became one of the most global of airliners of the post-war period, gaining sales in markets previously dominated by the big American aircraft manufacturers.

Strange as it may seem post-war aviation was high on the British Air Ministry's agenda when at the height of the Second World War, in 1942 to be precise, the Brabazon committee was formed. Lord Brabazon had been an aviation pioneer before becoming an MP and Minister for Aircraft Production in Churchill's wartime government. One of the recommendations made by his committee, when it reported in 1945, was two short to medium range airliners, the first a piston engined aircraft to replace the Douglas DC-3 and the second a new turboprop-powered aircraft, these aircraft being called the Types IIA and IIB.

In 1946 a contract was awarded to Vickers at Weybridge in Surrey and within two years the first prototype of the Vickers V630 Viscount had made its first flight. It handled well, gave an excellent performance and, equally important, the new Dart engines acted perfectly. However by this time Vickers had worked out that the aircraft would not be as economical to fly as they had first thought. By boosting the engine power, increasing the aircraft size and thereby adding more passengers the aircraft could fly faster and further but be economical at the same time. A prototype

of this V700 version was built and flew successfully in August 1950.

The Viscount's proposed first customer was British European Airways. Their enthusiasm was to be expected as, in the emerging civil aviation postwar world, the Viscount showed all the power, performance, safety, reliability and economies that were needed to make it a successful airliner.

BEA placed an order for 20 Viscounts, later increased to 26, and deliveries started in January 1953. By April of that same year the BEA Viscounts began

OPPOSITE
Air Canada, and its predecessor Trans-Canada Airlines, was the first North American Viscount operator and a prolific user of the type. Here is a Viscount at Malton in 1965

BELOW
A British European Airways Viscount refuels at Athens airport

VICKERS VISCOUNT

their first scheduled service to Cyprus via Rome and Athens.

Overseas orders started to arrive with the national carriers of France, Ireland, Canada and Australia all placing their faith in the aircraft. They were followed by Dutch airline KLM, British West Indian Airways, the Indian Air Force and Iraqi Airways but an order from the other side of the Atlantic was very special for Vickers. After the Big Four, TWA, American, United and Eastern, Capital Airlines was the United States' largest domestic carrier of the 1950s. In 1954 they ordered three Viscounts followed by further orders for 37 and 20. It was the first time that a major American airline had bought non-American manufactured aircraft.

New and better Viscounts were subsequently developed. The V800 series was made in many versions benefitting from Rolls Royce's constant ability to improve the Dart engines. More power meant more weight and more passengers could be carried.

One of the Viscount's biggest supporters was Trans Canada Airlines which later became Air Canada. At the beginning of TCA's relationship with Vickers there were no other turboprop aircraft flying in North America and passengers felt privileged to be transported in this modern quiet aircraft. In fact in 1958 TCA had a fleet of 51 Viscounts and flew the type right through to 1974.

By the time production of the Viscount stopped in 1964 more than 400 had been built. Perhaps more importantly they had been bought by more than 50 major airlines all over the World.

The Vickers Viscount was a real world beating, money earning, safe and reliable British airliner.

Chapter 22

Hawker Hunter

BELOW
Battle of Britain ace
and Hawker test pilot
Neville Duke in the
cockpit of a Hunter

If there is one company that has always been associated with the Royal Air Force's fighter force over its history it is Hawkers.

Harry Hawker and, amongst others, Tommy Sopwith, started the company in 1920 out of the ashes of the bankrupt Sopwith Aviation Company. Throughout the pre-Second World War years Hawker fighters such as the Fury, Demon and Hart equipped many squadrons in the UK and across the Empire. During the war many of those squadrons were initially re-equipped with Hawker Hurricanes, leading the defence of Britain alongside the Spitfire in 1940, and subsequently Typhoons and Tempests, two of the most powerful piston-engined aircraft ever built.

It was perhaps no surprise, therefore, when Hawker's chief designer, Sydney Camm, created a sleek, streamlined jet fighter to fit an Air Ministry specification

ABOVE
First production
Hunter F1 WT555

for a replacement for the Gloster Meteor. Many pilots say that if an aircraft looks right then it normally is right and the Hunter definitely falls into this category. Despite teething problems with firing its guns at high altitude the general design of the aircraft changed little through all its variants and years in service.

Pilots loved it. It was strong, handled well and was very stable which led to it becoming the aircraft of choice for aerobatics. Both 111 Squadron and subsequently 92 Squadron, the Black Arrows and the Blue Diamonds, flew the F.6 variant of the aircraft in their impressive aerobatic displays. In fact one of the highlights of air shows worldwide would have to be the Black Arrows' famous "22-ship loop" at the annual Farnborough Air Show in 1958.

The first prototype of the Hunter flew in July 1951 and at the controls was test pilot and decorated wartime fighter pilot, Neville Duke. Two years later he broke the world speed record reaching 727.63 mph in that same aircraft.

The Hunter started equipping the RAF's front-line fighter squadrons in the UK in 1954 and in its many variants stayed in service until 1976 when the ground attack version, the FGA9, was finally replaced by yet another Hawker aircraft, the sensational vertical take off Harrier.

One big issue with the Hunter was its low fuel load, a problem that could have

HAWKER HUNTER

ABOVE
Hawker Hunter WT594
was an early production
F.1 seen here on a test
flight

been simply fixed by the addition of an in-flight refuelling capability. Despite that the Hunter was hugely popular with its pilots, especially when the Mk.6 came into service in 1957. That year the Hunter force reached its zenith when 19 RAF squadrons were equipped with the Mk.6 alone.

The Hunter took part in many incursions and conflicts during its time as a frontline fighter. From escorting Canberra bombers during the Suez crisis in 1956 to ground attacks in Brunei, Aden and the Radfan they proved themselves equal to the task.

The Hawker Hunter was favoured by many air forces round the world. When many of the Hunters built as fighters were withdrawn by air forces they were acquired by Hawkers and converted to ground attack versions for the Royal Air Force and many other countries. Eventually variants were used by the Royal Air Force, Royal Navy and no less than 21 other countries including Switzerland, India, Jordan and Singapore. Lebanon is now the final air force still using active Hunters.

Hunters are still hugely popular at air

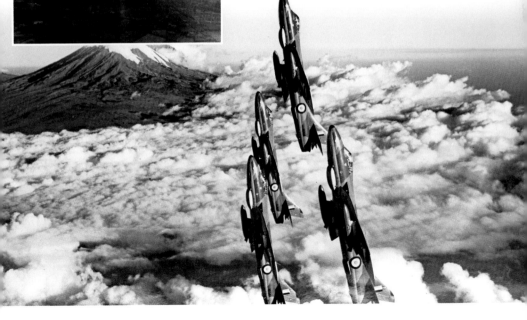

shows across the world. At the 50th anniversary celebrations for the aircraft at Kemble in Gloucestershire in 2001 a rare treat for the crowds was a delta formation of 15 Hunters, a sight seldom seen since the aircraft's heyday in the 1950s.

LEFT
The incredible 22 ship loop by 111 Squadron's Black Arrows Hunter display team at Farnborough in 1958

BELOW
Four Hunter FGA.9s climb with Mount Kenya in the distance

Chapter 23

Hunting-Percival Jet Provost

As jet aircraft were introduced into the Royal Air Force during the 1940s and early 1950s it became obvious that a pure piston-engined training course was no preparation for flying the much faster front line jet fighters and bombers. The leap in performance was just too great. At one point it was not unusual for one third of newly qualified pilots, initially trained on a combination of piston-engined aircraft, to be rejected by Operational Conversion Units as unsuitable for flying jets.

So even as new training aircraft such as the Hunting Percival Provost entered service the Royal Air Force began searching for its first jet trainer. Hunting Percival had already foreseen this requirement and

ABOVE
A Jet Provost T.3 from
the RAF's 1FTS at
Leeming in 1980

designed an aircraft for that specific role.

The Jet Provost first flew in June 1954 and instantly proved to be a hit with the RAF. Nine of these T.1 aircraft were ordered mainly because of their superb handling qualities and a side-by-side layout. They proved successful in their trials and in 1959 the RAF ordered upgraded variants which became the standard basic jet trainer and stayed in service for the next 35 years.

The Royal Air Force used the Jet Provost, or 'JP' as it became known, in many of their training flights and schools but perhaps the most important was the Central Flying School based at various times at Little Rissington in Gloucestershire, Cranwell, Leeming and Scampton. CFS trains military flying instructors and its main training aircraft for 34 years was the Jet Provost.

It was at CFS that the RAF's first Jet Provost display team, The Sparrows, was formed in 1958. They were followed by The Redskins and eventually the most famous JP team of them all, The Red

ABOVE
A Jet Provost T.4 of the RAF's College of Air Warfare's display team 'The Macaws' seen at Hatfield in 1968

RIGHT
Four Jet Provost T.5s from 6FTS at RAF Finningley flying over the Fylingdales 'golf balls' early warning radar station in Yorkshire

Pelicans in 1962. Not to be outdone No. 1 Flying Training School (1FTS) formed the Gin Four and then The Blades. The College of Air Warfare had The Macaws while 3FTS flew The Swords and the Royal Air Force College Cranwell The Poachers. All these teams proved that the Jet Provost was one of the most stable, easy to handle and perfect aerobatic aircraft the RAF ever had. In fact there were more display teams formed on Jet Provosts than any other aircraft in the RAF's history.

When Hunting Percival was absorbed into the British Aircraft Corporation in 1959 the new company expanded the scope of the Jet Provost. As a trainer it had already been adopted by countries as far afield as Kuwait, Venezuela and Sri Lanka. Now BAC fitted more powerful engines and turned the aircraft into an efficient and cost effective light attack aircraft which was bought by Saudi Arabia, Kenya, Singapore and many other air forces round the world. Almost 150 of these Strikemasters, as they were called, were manufactured.

Now, 60 years after its first flight, there are many JPs still flying in private ownership. However it will always be known as the aircraft that introduced jet training to the Royal Air Force.

Chapter 24

Avro Vulcan

For some it's the sheer size and the distinctive shape or the manoeuvrability of this enormous aircraft in flight. For others it's the power as the last remaining airworthy example takes to the skies with its engines screaming. For many, though, it is the role the Vulcan played in the darkest days of the Cold War when she helped to keep the peace between the West and the Soviet Union.

RIGHT
An Avro 707A research aircraft undertaking high speed testing for the future Avro Vulcan nuclear bomber

OPPOSITE
Avro Vulcan bombers under construction

Avro built thousands of aircraft; trainers such as the 504; airliners such as the York and Tudor; but their single biggest contribution to British aviation history was heavy bombers, the Lancaster and Lincoln.

It was therefore no surprise when the design tendered by Avro to provide a strategic nuclear bomber for the RAF was considered as way ahead of those offered by other manufacturers.

Roy Chadwick had led the team that created the Lancaster and it was his original design for the enormous delta wing Vulcan that so impressed the Air Ministry. Chadwick and his chief designer, Stuart Duncan Davies, studied the research on swept wing aircraft captured from German scientists towards the end of the war and created the shape that became so famous in the Vulcan.

Sadly Chadwick was killed in an airliner crash in 1947 but Davies continued and developed the design that won a contract later that same year. None of the other tenders for the contract were as risky as the Vulcan so smaller sized test aircraft were built. These Avro 707s proved that the shape worked and that the vast delta wing would give fighter style manoeuvrability as well as the lift

AVRO VULCAN

necessary to make the aircraft work.

Avro chief test pilot Roly Falk took the prototype Vulcan for its first flight on 30 August 1952. Just a week later, at the SBAC show at Farnborough, he astonished the crowd by rolling the aircraft, not something was allowed to happen in public again.

It was almost exactly 10 years after the death of Roy Chadwick when the first RAF Vulcan squadron, number 83,

took delivery of its aircraft. These were Mark 1 aircraft, painted anti-flash white, and their arrival coincided with that of Yellow Sun, Britain's first true nuclear weapon, a parachute bomb which was to be dropped by the Vulcans from a great height.

By 1960 there were four Vulcan squadrons but already the Mark 1 was being phased out to be replaced by the Mark 2. Visually there was a different shape to the wings and there was a larger tail fairing carrying new radar. However inside a change of engine meant that the Vulcan now had a substantially increased range and could fly higher and faster on its chosen mission.

This was the height of the Cold War. The Soviet Union was the great enemy and the Vulcans' job was to obliterate Moscow and other Soviet cities with their nuclear bombs, a task that caused more than a few crew to reconsider their beliefs! They also had a new weapon to carry. Blue Steel was manufactured by Avro and was Britain's first nuclear missile.

Only once did the Vulcan ever have to go to war and that was with conventional bombs. By the late 1970s the Vulcans had outlived their purpose. The nuclear deterrent had passed to the Royal Navy's submarines and the RAF was bringing new aircraft into service. However the war in the Falklands in 1982 gave the Vulcan a chance to shine.

Four Vulcans successfully launched a series of attacks against Argentine forces and Port Stanley airport in support of ground operations.

Now there is just one of these majestic aircraft left flying. Supported by public donation XH558 continues to thrill crowds at air shows and let people see one of the aircraft that defended Britain during the Cold war.

BELOW
Vulcan B.2 XH534 flying at Farnborough in 1960

Handley Page Victor

Handley Page built many types of aircraft but foremost was heavy bombers. In the First World War it was the 0/100, 0/400 and eventually the V/1500.

In the Second World War it was the Hampden and Halifax but Handley Page

still had one further big bomber design up its sleeve, the Victor.

Designs for three different bombers were chosen to form Britain's airborne nuclear deterrent in the darkest days of the Cold War of which the Victor was the third.

The Air Ministry issued their specification as early as January 1947 and four contenders were chosen from the designs tendered. The Handley Page design showed an aircraft with a crescent shaped wing and an unusually shaped cockpit, just two areas of radical design which led the Air Ministry to order a 40% size research aircraft, the HP88. The loss of this aircraft just two months after its first flight did not affect the programme as Handley Page had forged ahead with the construction of two prototypes for the Victor.

In December 1952 one of the aircraft was broken down at the Handley Page factory in Radlett and carried by road to Boscombe Down where it flew for the first time on Christmas Eve. The aircraft went into production and the first emerged from the factory for its first flight on 1 February 1956.

10 Squadron RAF, based at Cottesmore, was the first to receive the Victor in April 1958 with 15 Squadron following in September and 57 Squadron in January 1959.

Handley Page now turned their full attention to developing a more powerful variant. The RAF wanted their bombers to fly even higher so Handley Page built bigger wings and introduced the Rolls Royce Conway engine for the B.2 which entered service in 1962.

ABOVE
Line up of Victor B.1 bombers at the Handley Page factory in Radlett

HANDLEY PAGE VICTOR

The future of the V-Force was thrown into doubt when US pilot Gary Powers was shot down by a Soviet missile while flying a U2 spyplane over the Soviet Union in 1960. He was flying at nearly 70,000 feet which was much higher than any of the V-bombers could fly and instantly destroyed any idea that the V-Force was invulnerable to Soviet defences. When the US built Skybolt missile was cancelled and Polaris was ordered which would transfer the nuclear deterrent to the Royal Navy, it was obvious that the V-Force would lose its main role within a few years.

Handley Page had their orders reduced and 28 of the B.2 Victors were cancelled.

21 of the B.2s were refitted to B.2R standard with even more powerful engines so that they could carry the British-built Blue Steel nuclear weapon but a change in RAF policy meant that the bombers would have to carry their bomb loads at low-level rather than the ultra high level for which the aircraft had been built.

The Vickers Valiant was withdrawn in 1965 because of metal fatigue leaving the RAF with no tanker in service. The Victor B.1s were all hastily refitted and emerged as tankers before the end of 1966.

The last bombers were withdrawn in 1968 and the B.2Rs were converted to tankers.

HANDLEY PAGE VICTOR

The Victor had led a troubled life in its short few years in service as a bomber but this was totally due to political issues and strategic policy than any problems with the aircraft. From 1968 onwards the Victor proved itself as a vital part of the RAF's fleet and stayed in service longer than either of the other two V-Force aircraft. In 1982 Victors provided the refuelling required to get the Vulcan bombers to the Falkland Islands and bomb the Port Stanley airport runway. Again in 1991 Victors were used during the Gulf War, a successful swansong before they were withdrawn in 1993, the heaviest load carrying and longest serving bomber in RAF history.

LEFT
XL164's nose art...
'Saucy Sal'

BELOW
An RAF Victor K.2
after landing

Chapter 26

Vickers VC10

'L isten to the hushed voice of luxury' said the BOAC advertisement for jet travel in their VC10 airliners. 'Try a little VC10derness" was another. And this was just one of the reasons why the VC10 became a favourite of the British public and pilots alike.

Hugely successful though they were Vickers were disappointed when their V1000 jet airliner proposal came to nothing in the mid 1950s. It had been based on the RAF's first V bomber, the Valiant, to be a strategic transport aircraft for Britain's armed forces and then a civil jet airliner. The RAF lost interest, BOAC were already committed to the Comet 4 and the Britannia and just months before the proposed first flight the V1000 was

cancelled. Within a year BOAC realised that neither of their new aircraft would fulfill the needs of long range international jet travel and ordered Boeing 707s from America. Any lead that Britain had in jet aircraft manufacture disappeared and was taken by the United States.

In March 1957 BOAC issued a specification for an even longer range aircraft than the 707. This was needed to fly the African and Australian routes and would need to be capable of taking off and land-

ing at high altitudes and in hot countries. Vickers had already experimented with a design based on four rear-mounted engines and now this design was tailored to meet BOAC's requirements. Almost instantly the benefits of the Vickers design seemed to mirror the needs of BOAC. A flight from Lagos to London via the Nigerian town of Kano is a good example of what the VC10 would need to deal with; taking off from the dense humidity of Lagos and landing on the

Not quite snowbound!
VC10 G-ARVC on a
snowy December day
at Heathrow airport
in 1964

short runway at Kano, 500 metres above sea level, in temperatures in excess of thirty centigrade before flying 2,514 miles to London. Allowing for the fact that this new aircraft could also fly the transatlantic routes BOAC signed a contract for 35 VC10s in January 1958.

Even as these first VC10s were being built Vickers developed a longer and higher capacity version called the Super VC10 so

now there were two versions available; the 'standard' which carried 135 passengers and the 'Super' with up to 212 seats.

Passengers and crew alike enjoyed their VC10 experience with pilots finding it an easy aircraft to fly and passengers revelling in the quiet and comfortable cabin. Surely the VC10 would become a worldwide success?

Vickers received a few more orders,

mostly from Commonwealth countries such as Ghana, Nigeria and Ceylon but by this time the huge US manufacturers such as Boeing and Douglas dominated the international market with cheaper and more economical aircraft. Statistics don't usually lie and in this case the manufacturing figures show the stark reality of US dominance. 54 VC10s and Super VC10s were built while more than 1000 Boeing 707s graced the skies.

Although the VC10s were successful at BOAC they rapidly went out of service by 1974 with the Super VC10s following just six years later. However the aircraft enjoyed a substantially longer life in Royal Air Force service. 14 were ordered for the RAF and were initially used as transports carrying up to 150 troops, and potentially their families, so the cabins were equipped to a similar standard as for civil flights. In 1984 the RAF began to get further VC10s to be used as tankers, these being aircraft being acquired from various operating airlines. In this refuelling role the aircraft stayed in service until the autumn of 2013, more than 50 years after the type's first flight.

This classic, luxurious and capable aircraft was to be the last aircraft ever designed and manufactured solely by Vickers as the company became part of the merged British Aircraft Corporation in 1960.

BELOW
RAF VC10 K.4 tanker
ZD242 at its home base
at RAF Brize Norton

Chapter 27

English Electric Lightning

RIGHT
English Electric
Lightning F.2s of 74
Squadron's display
team 'The Tigers'

Speed has always been a vital part in the armoury of any front-line fighter aircraft. In the Cold War world of fast jets the ability to take off and intercept enemy aircraft well away from the homeland was essential Until the English Electric Lightning took to the skies RAF front-line fighters such as the Hawker Hunter only managed to fly supersonic in a dive. With the coming of the Lightning the RAF gained its first genuine supersonic fighter. In fact by the time the aircraft had been fully developed its top speed was Mach 2.27 or 1,500mph.

The Lightning was designed by WEW 'Teddy' Petter, his last design for English Electric before he left to work at Folland.

It started as a set of proposals for research into supersonic flight and sat alongside a similar project researching air-to-air guided missiles that it was expected a supersonic fighter would carry.

The Lightning began life as the P.1A prototype which first flew in 1954. Chief test pilot Roly Beamont was pleased with the handling of the aircraft but one area of concern would plague the aircraft throughout its service life, a chronically short endurance.

Over the next five years many more prototypes and development aircraft were built leading to the first production Lightning F. Mk.1 which flew in November

It could fly twice as fast as any previous aircraft, higher at 60,000ft and was a genuine next generation fighter with its integrated radar and armament controls. It also had an amazing climb rate meaning it could be at interception height far quicker than any previous fighter. Its one achilles heel was its endurance. A fast climb to great height could reduce the endurance of the aircraft to barely 40 minutes. This problem was solved in later variants by the addition of extra jettisonable external fuel tanks.

The Lightning's role in the Royal Air Force was as a pure interceptor in the air defence of the United Kingdom and various overseas countries. Many times Lightnings were scrambled to intercept the new generation of Soviet bombers patrolling over the North Cape and gently shepherd them away from British skies.

1959 and entered service with the Royal Air Force in June 1960.

The Lightning provided the RAF with a quantum leap in fighter performance.

74 Squadron was the first ever Lightning squadron and was given the role

of bringing this hugely powerful aircraft into service. Its CO Sqn. Ldr. John Howe was also given the unenviable task of providing a nine-ship Lightning display team at the same time, one they achieved barely three months after the aircraft went into service when the squadron performed at the Farnborough Air Show. Getting to know these new aircraft was a difficult task and it was sheer professionalism that meant the squadron successfully achieved both tasks. Later 74 Squadron was deployed for seven years to Tengah in the defence of Singapore, the first time a

Lightning squadron went abroad. Other squadrons defended RAF bases in Germany and Cyprus.

The ultimate version of the Lightning, the F. Mk.6, remained on the front line well into the 1980s when it was replaced by the next generation of fighters, the Tornado F.3.

Throughout its RAF service the Lightning was a spectacular performer at airshows. After 74 Squadron "Tigers" thrilled crowds for three years the mantle of RAF display squadron went to 56 Squadron, the Firebirds. The aircraft was still wowing audiences more than 20 years later in its final years of service.

BELOW
One of the last
Lightning F.6 aircraft
of the LTF in 1987

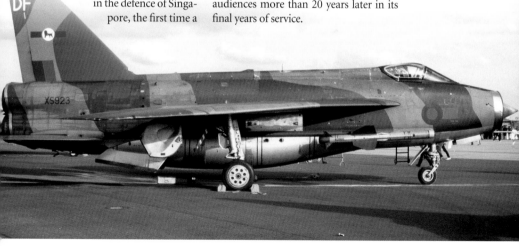

Chapter 28

Folland Gnat

One aircraft designer who deserves more recognition is WEW "Teddy" Petter, the man responsible for the Lysander while he worked at Westland and the classic Canberra and P.1, forerunner of the Lightning, at English Electric.

Petter was concerned about the increasing cost and size of fighters and wanted to pursue designs for lighter and more cost effective aircraft. He resigned from English Electric and joined Folland Aircraft in 1950 replacing Henry Folland as managing director the following year.

Petter's first lightweight design was for a single seat fighter called the Midge which flew for the first time in August 1954. The next version, now re-engined and renamed the Gnat, flew the following year. It received no RAF orders as they chose the Hunter to fulfill the proposed Gnat role.

Despite the lack of interest for the single seat Gnat from the RAF, Petter continued development of a two-seat version. The increasing complexity of RAF frontline aircraft meant that more advanced trainers were needed. In the late 1950s the training for fast jet cadets was from the Jet Provost to the Vampire T.11 and onto an Operational Conversion Unit. However the difference in performance between the Vampire and aircraft like the Hunter meant that trainees had to relearn flying techniques let alone methods of air warfare. A faster trainer would be needed and the Gnat suited the purpose.

14 pre-production aircraft were or-dered in 1958 and the first flight of the two-seat Gnat took place on 31 August 1959.

The Gnat T.Mk.1 that entered service with the RAF in early 1962 differed from the original single seater in just a few ways. Slightly bigger wings for larger fuel tanks and a longer fuselage to accommo-date the two seats were the main changes but internally the changes were radical. The cockpit had to contain virtually all the equipment that was used by the frontline aircraft of the time including the brand new Lightning. This meant a complete redesign of the cockpit and all its instrumentation.

The six trials Gnats that arrived at the

FOLLAND GNAT

Central Flying School could fly at 40,000 feet and could go supersonic in a dive. At the same time they could fly well at the low speeds suitable for a novice jet pilot. It was sensitive to fly but provided a much better performance than the Jet Provost. It also gave instructors an aircraft that would really pose their students a challenge and prepare them for flying those fast frontline jets.

It was no surprise perhaps when these new trainers were chosen to form a display team for the 1964 season. The Yellowjacks were soon followed by the Red Arrows which flew the type for a further 15 years.

Although some more Gnats were delivered to CFS the majority went to Valley to equip 4FTS and replace the Vampire T.11s. Although it fulfilled all the RAF's requirements there were still a few issues, most of which related to the size of the aircraft. Tall pilots simply couldn't fit and if they did, and had to eject, they were liable to suffer leg injuries. Whilst easy to maintain ground crew did find they could be fiddly with so much equipment packed into a small space.

The Gnat stayed in service until phased out from 1978 and finally replaced completely by the Hawk. 4FTS graduated its final course of students in November 1979 and the Gnat was officially gone.

Considering how hard these aircraft were flown in RAF service, there are still plenty of Gnats flying around the world. At least 15 of the 200 built still fly and many more grace museums and airfields around the world.

Blackburn Buccaneer

The early 1950s was a dangerous time for Britain's Royal Navy. Faced with a growing threat from the expanding Soviet fleet they needed an aircraft that could attack and sink these Soviet ships. Blackburn Aircraft, based at Brough near Hull, had built a reputation for building naval aircraft including biplane torpedo bombers between the wars and carrier-borne wartime dive bombers, the Skua and Roc.

The Blackburn Buccaneer came from a need for a low-level, carrier-borne strike aircraft capable of delivering both conventional and nuclear weapons. As always with carrier aircraft it needed to be robust in both the airframe and the undercarriage which would also help cope with the extra stress of flying low.

20 prototypes were built, each one adding a further piece of the jigsaw that would end up as an extremely capable jet bomber. One included the folding wings,

another an innovative revolving bomb bay and one added the refuelling probe. All were powered by the de Havilland Gyron Junior engine and featured the folding nose and extended rear fuselage which opened as air brakes. These two features also meant that this long aircraft

could just fit on the lifts fitted on carriers to raise and lower aircraft from the lower decks.

The first Buccaneer flew on 30 April 1958 and within two years production aircraft were being delivered to the Royal Navy trials unit. In July 1962 801 NAS

became the first Fleet Air Arm squadron to receive Buccaneers. 801 was commanded by the then Lt. Cdr. Ted Anson who had been one of the original Buccaneer test pilots and would go on to become captain of HMS Ark Royal and end up as a Vice Admiral and Flag Officer of the Naval Air Command.

These Mark 1 aircraft operated successfully with the Royal Navy for nine years but they were underpowered which meant that each aircraft had to take off with a smaller fuel load to reduce weight and then be refuelled by a Buccaneer tanker. In response Blackburn built a Mark 2 variant with more powerful Rolls Royce Spey engines and these replaced the Mark 1 in the late 1960s.

The Buccaneer had originally been offered to the RAF to fill their need for a low-level nuclear bomber but it had been rejected in favour of their new advanced strike aircraft, TSR2, being built by BAC but in 1965 it was cancelled. The plan was to buy a version of the American F-111 swing-wing bomber instead but this was also cancelled. At the same time the future of the Navy's aircraft carriers was decided so the Royal Navy would have Buccaneers available. 62 ex-Fleet Air Arm Buccaneers were transferred to the RAF alongside 26 new ones. The first RAF squadron, number 12, began operating Buccaneers in 1969.

RAF Buccaneer squadrons undertook a variety of roles over the next 20 years including anti-shipping, laser targeting, conventional and nuclear bombing based initially in mainland Britain extending to become part of RAF Germany as well. By 1991 the Buccaneer was disappearing from service but the Gulf War changed that. Unable to designate their own targets the Tornado squadrons deployed to the Gulf needed the assistance of the Buccaneers fitted with their Pave Spike laser targeting pods. Buccaneers successfully marked targets for their own Paveway laser bombs as well as those of the Tornados proving that this 40 year-old design still had a role to play in a modern battlefield.

BELOW
Proving the longevity of the Buccaneer a Gulf War veteran from 208 Squadron's 'Sky Pirates' on display at Fairford in 1991

BAC One Eleven

While long-haul flights may have had the glamour of flying to distant parts of the world, often the most profitable and most keenly fought over were the short-haul routes.

Efficient, cost-effective and reliable aircraft were always needed for these routes and in the BAC One Eleven the world's airlines found one. The only European competition for this market was from the Sud Aviation Caravelle which had entered service with Air France in 1959.

In 1960 one of the newly formed British Aircraft Corporation's first decisions was to choose a design to replace the Vickers Viscount. BAC benefitted from all the experience of the teams that had built the Viscount, VC10 and Britannia. Added to that was a new concept from Hunting Aircraft and the BAC One Eleven was born.

Traditionally a British airliner was built to a specification from an airline such as BOAC. Without this BAC were

able to create a design free from restrictions and so could attract airlines all over the world. The aircraft that was launched in 1961 had up to 80 seats and two Rolls Royce Spey engines. It could fly 500 to 800 mile sectors which made it ideal for short haul routes all over the world.

Even before the first flight BAC received orders. The new British United Airways was the first customer followed rapidly by Braniff and Mohawk, two important regional American airlines. By the time the aircraft first flew on 20 August 1963 BAC held orders for 60 aircraft and even the crash of the prototype in October 1963 didn't affect the likelihood of success.

One of the secrets of BAC's success was the commercial lead they had over their nearest rival, the Douglas DC-9. Douglas

was lagging behind which meant that the American government was not able to invoke an agreement whereby they could ban a US airline from buying foreign aircraft if a suitable American alternative existed.

BAC were able to deliver their first aircraft in late 1964, the same year the DC-9 flew for the first time. BAC had been well ahead but they were taken by surprise with the speed that Douglas caught up and by their range of standard and stretched versions. With such a variety of aircraft on offer sales of the DC-9 rocketed until by the end of 1966 Douglas had orders for 400 aircraft.

Unfortunately the existing Spey engine was not powerful enough to cope with a bigger One Eleven so it was 1967 before BAC could offer their own stretched version, the One Eleven 500. Sales continued slowly for the next few years but by then the DC-9 competitor had been joined by the Boeing 737 and when production of the aircraft halted in 1982 the BAC factory had delivered 235 aircraft, that's almost as many as the total sales of the VC10, Britannia and Trident together.

There was one short re-emergence of the One Eleven when Romania signed an agreement to manufacture the aircraft,

called the ROMBAC One Eleven, under license. Unfortunately the Romanian economy was unable to cope with the cash flow required and the supply of components ground to a halt. Just nine aircraft were built.

Throughout the 1970s and 80s BAC One Elevens provided great service for a multitude of airlines. Many independents flew them in the UK and when most of them disappeared British Airways were so pleased with the service offered that they bought more new 500 series One Elevens for their internal UK routes. The last BAC One Eleven in Britain was retired as recently as 2012.

Chapter 31

BAC TSR2

Just a single aircraft actually flew and only for six months. It never entered service and was cancelled due to to its high projected costs. However TSR2, the prototype that never even got a name, was perhaps one of the most influential aircraft of all time and its cancellation has been one of the most bitterly discussed decisions in British aviation history.

The late 1950s and early 1960s was a perilous time for the aviation industry worldwide as costs soared and profits became very hard to find. Aircraft companies could not rely on the civil market alone and the newly formed British Aircraft Corporation was searching for a military counter to the VC10 and

BAC1-11 airliners, neither of which had proven themselves as money spinners at that time.

BAC was formed in 1960 by the merger of aviation giants Vickers-Armstrongs and English Electric together with Bristol Aircraft. However Vickers and English Electric had already been jointly awarded the contract to build the TSR2 a year earlier. TSR2, standing for Tactical Strike Reconnaissance, was officially planned to be the replacement for the Canberra but the actual specification was hugely more complicated. From its name alone it was obvious it would have strike and reconnaissance roles but it also had to fly supersonic, in all weather at low level, day or night, and penetrate some of the world's most sophisticated defences to deliver a nuclear weapon. It had to be able to carry a wide range of nuclear and conventional weapons, use terrain-following radar, take off from short and rough airstrips, and have a bewildering set of computers to run virtually every function.

It was a huge challenge and was not going to be cheap. Initially TSR2 was due to be in service by 1965 but the rising cost of all that new technology and constant

OPPOSITE
TSR2 flight crew, pilot Roland Beamont and navigator Donald Bowen, prepare for the first flight at Boscombe Down on 27 September 1964

ABOVE
TSR2 first engine runs in May 1964

ABOVE
TSR2 XR219 on one of
its early test flights

delays in decision making by government committees meant that soon the aircraft was behind schedule.

While the RAF wanted, and BAC seemed able to deliver, a state-of-the-art military aircraft the British Treasury became one of the most vocal, but by no means the only, opponents. The Royal Navy, championed by Lord Mountbatten, wanted the RAF to share in the cost of their new Blackburn Buccaneer low-level nuclear strike bombers. In fact Mountbatten was almost single-handedly responsible for persuading the Royal Australian Air Force not to buy TSR2, a contract which would surely have saved the aircraft from oblivion. The USA wanted to sell the RAF their new F-111

swing-wing bombers and actively opposed TSR2's continuing development and when the new Labour government was voted in with a slim majority in 1964 TSR2 was doomed.

At that point the aircraft had flown very successfully. Test pilot Roland Beamont had taken it into the air for the first time in September 1964. On the 14th flight on 12 March 1965 Beamont went supersonic and the data from these flights built up to be a valuable source for the future. However at the annual budget statement on 6 April 1965 TSR2 was cancelled officially due to cost. BAC wanted to continue with test flying to gather even more data to be used in the development of Concorde but permission was refused.

Two prototypes were saved, one is now at RAF Cosford and one at the Imperial War Museum at Duxford, but all the jigs, tools and remaining aircraft were to be destroyed.

Sir Sydney Camm summed up the industry's feelings about TSR2. "All modern aircraft have four dimensions: span, length, height and politics. TSR2 simply got the first three right."

BELOW
A dramatic night shot of TSR2 after being rolled out from its hangar

Chapter 32

Hawker Harrier

In 1957 Dr Stanley Hooker, technical director of Bristol Engines, approached Hawkers with a radical idea to develop an aircraft for their new Pegasus engine which could provide the ability to take off and land vertically. Hawkers took on the project as their hugely successful Hunter was nearing the end of its development life and the proposed replacement had been cancelled by the British Government.

It may seem obvious now but the benefits of vertical and short take off and landing, or V-STOL, technology are many. Armed forces can operate from smaller ships and smaller landing grounds. In fact they can land, refuel and rearm much closer to the front line providing almost constant sup-

port to ground forces.

In just three years the Hawker team led by a thirty one year old designer, Ralph Hooper, under the chief designer Sir Sydney Camm developed a revolutionary aircraft, the P.1127, which was flown for the first time on 21 October 1960. Test pilot Bill Bedford was a wartime pilot who had spent most of his post-RAF career at Hawkers testing Hunters. Now faced with the radically different P.1127 V-STOL prototype he had to develop an entirely new method of flying a fixed wing aircraft which could hover like a helicopter while still act like a traditional fighter aircraft in flight. Bedford raised the aircraft to just a few inches off the ground in a tethered hover and a new age of flight was born.

OPPOSITE
A Spanish Harrier, called an HR.1 Matador, flies alongside an RAF aircraft

ABOVE
Sea Harrier FA.2 XZ495 of 899 Squadron FAA on board an aircraft carrier in 1992

HAWKER HARRIER

The next stage of development from the P.1127 prototypes was the production of nine Kestrel aircraft, three for each of the United States, UK and West Germany. These were then used to evaluate the performance and potential of the technology. When the Kestrels had successfully completed their testing the first Harriers went into production.

The Harrier GR1 entered service with the Royal Air Force in 1969. It was heavily deployed as part of RAF Germany and became the RAF's major close support and ground attack aircraft. It would have been the first line of defence against Soviet tanks advancing across the European battlefield.

The other major operator of the Harrier was the US Marine Corps where it was designated the AV-8A.

It was USMC operations at sea that persuaded other countries to buy the Harrier. Thailand, Spain and India all operated the aircraft from their carriers but it was a completely new version, the Sea Harrier, that entered service with Britain's Royal Navy. They flew alongside RAF Harriers in their most high profile operation, the Falklands War of 1982, where they provided air defence for the fleet as well as joining the RAF in ground attack operations.

Shortage of money slowed the UK development of an advanced Harrier but British Aerospace's partner McDonnell Douglas pushed ahead creating the Harrier II. Using composite materials and saving weight in construction the Harrier II was able to improve performance, this more powerful aircraft carrying a heavier and more varied payload.

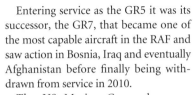

Entering service as the GR5 it was its successor, the GR7, that became one of the most capable aircraft in the RAF and saw action in Bosnia, Iraq and eventually Afghanistan before finally being withdrawn from service in 2010.

The US Marine Corps, however, continue to operate their AV-8Bs and current plans seem likely to extend their lives for many more years to come due partly to delays in the replacement F-35B Lightning II programme but also because the Harriers are still relevant and capable aircraft.

LEFT
A US Marine Corps
AV-8B in 1981

BELOW
Live firing exercise
for an RAF Harrier

Chapter 33

Concorde

If there was ever a milestone in flight performance and profile it was the joint venture Aerospatiale and British Aircraft Corporation's Concorde.

Fabulous to watch, iconic in design and supersonic in flight, Concorde revolutionised business and commercial flying.

For years it was possible to leave London in the morning and watch the sun rise as Concorde arrived in New York. It halved the flight time from London to New York to three and a half hours as it flew its 100 passengers at up to 1350 mph across the Atlantic. At that speed it covered a mile every 2.75 seconds which meant that passengers arrived in New York at least an hour before they had departed due to time zone differences.

A project like Concorde takes a very long time to get from the original idea to flight.

From the early 1950s British committees and groups studied all manner of research into wing and engine design to see whether it would be possible to build a supersonic commercial airliner.

Similar research was underway in France so under an agreement signed in 1962 the two countries worked together. Almost immediately both the USA and Soviet Union announced that they were planning supersonic transports. The USA never managed to make their plans work and the aircraft was eventually cancelled in 1971. The Soviet-built Tupolev Tu-144, however, came to fruition and actu-

ally flew before the Anglo-French aircraft. 'Concordski', as it became known, was a serious rival but an aircraft crashed while displaying at the Paris Air Show in 1973 and the whole project ended in 1978.

The French prototype Concorde flew for the first time on 2 March 1969 with the British aircraft following just a month later. For the next few years the aircraft spent their time testing and flying on sales trips around the World. There was huge interest in the supersonic airliner from many countries but events conspired to stop Concorde from becoming a huge financial success alongside its technical triumph.

OPPOSITE
The beautiful silhouette of a British Airways Concorde

ABOVE
British Airways Concorde G-BOAE currently displayed at Granley Adams Airport in Barbados

The Concordski crash in 1973, spiralling costs and the world oil crisis persuaded many prospective buyers to drop out but delays in the approval of routes to the USA because of environmental concerns perhaps finally put an end to Concorde's potential as a world-beater.

The outcome was that only 20 Concordes were ever built of which six were prototypes and the rest were flown either by British Airways or Air France.

It would be unfair to focus solely on the problems that Concorde endured through its development and introduction into service. Despite the setbacks the most technically advanced aviation concept in the world up to that time was actually completed in an age when virtually every other new aircraft was cancelled, surviving the various political shenanigans of governments from both sides. It took no longer to go from the drawing board to reality than any equivalent subsonic design and it stayed in service for 27 years carry-

ing more than four million passengers.

Charter passengers enjoyed trips to the Pyramids in Egypt and fly / sail holidays to New York returning on the QE2 cruise liner. Concorde flew to over 150 destinations around the World and was regularly used in celebrations and flypasts, often in formation with the RAF's Red Arrows. Concorde became the choice of the rich and famous with passenger lists regularly including heads of State, film stars and prominent politicians.

But all good things have to come to an end. In July 2000 an Air France Concorde crashed near Paris and all aircraft were grounded. Commercial flights resumed in November 2001 but by then other factors conspired to end Concorde's flying days.

9/11; rising fuel prices; increased maintenance costs for these ageing aircraft; and a refusal by Airbus to continue maintenance support. For these reasons the first age of commercial supersonic flight came to an end in 2003.

BELOW
With speed and streamlined design came a cramped passenger cabin. Here the interior of G-BOAC

Chapter 34

Hawker
Siddeley Hawk

The story of the Hawk is one of problem-free development from the experienced team at Hawker Siddeley

based at the historic Hawker building in Kingston in Surrey. The team, led by ex-Folland designer Gordon Hodson, knew there would only be one new trainer for the RAF and it would stay in service for many years so it would be a valuable contract to win. A combat capability was to be attached to the new aircraft which would increase the chances of international success as well.

The specification from the Ministry of Defence came in 1970. Hawker Siddeley had started on their design as a private venture in 1968 and the RAF had worked closely with the design team. Almost unique in British aviation the Ministry of Defence placed an order for 175 Hawks before the aircraft had been tested or even flown!

Hawker Siddeley test pilot Duncan Simpson flew the Hawk for the first time on 21 August 1974. It was a stable, comfortable aircraft. It had a good field of vision which was vital for a trainee pilot, and it handled well within the spinning and stalling requirements of the RAF. Equally important it was cost effective to build and to maintain.

Just a few days later Simpson took the aircraft to Farnborough for the air show. In awful weather he flew it throughout the eight days of the 1974 show.

The Hawk provided exactly what the Royal Air Force needed at that time. As cockpits became more complex then the training needed to provide that level of complexity. The Hawk achieved this by

go supersonic in a dive and had great endurance. The Royal Air Force had a terrific new jet trainer that would last them well beyond the end of the 20th Century.

For five years from 1976 the RAF's new Hawks were delivered to training schools all over the country. First to get them was No.4 Flying Training School at RAF Valley on Anglesey in North Wales. For more than fifty years generations of RAF fast jet pilots have graduated from 4 FTS and gone on to fly everything from the Lightning to the Tornado and Typhoon.

In the late 70s the Gnats flown by the Red Arrows were beginning to show their age. It was time to change over to the RAF's latest jet trainer. In 1979 the Central Flying School took delivery of the team's aircraft and the Red Arrows were ready to work up their routine during the winter of 1979 / 80.

As soon as the Hawk was established with the RAF Hawker Siddeley was on the search for export orders. Finland, Kenya and Indonesia were the first customers for the Hawk 50, the initial export version. In the early 1980s the next version, the Hawk 60, attracted orders from the Middle East as well as South Korea, Zimbabwe and Switzerland.

The Hawk 100, a weapons trainer with

providing a similar cockpit layout to that of the front line aircraft.

The Hawk could climb fast and could

advanced avionics, secured interest from the Middle East and Malaysia together with a Canadian order for the CT-155 Hawk.

The Hawk is still the most successful jet trainer aircraft in the world. Almost 1,000 have been sold and they are in service with thirteen countries. Perhaps the most important overseas agreement is with the United States.

In 1978 British Aerospace and McDonnell Douglas jointly developed the T-45 Goshawk as a carrier-borne jet trainer for the US Navy. 125 T-45As were ordered and now, more than thirty years later, the T-45C is still providing advanced training to US naval aviators.

OPPOSITE
Perhaps the best advertisement for the Hawk is the RAF's famous display team the Red Arrows

BELOW
The Red Arrows' Hawk T.1s fly past the White Cliffs of Dover

Chapter 35

Panavia Tornado

I t is unusual but by no means unique for a company to be formed to produce a single aircraft. But Panavia was just such a company.

It was the 1960s. The Cold War was at its height and the countries of Western Europe were the front line. Battle scenarios were played again and again to see what might happen if the Soviet Union attacked.

At the heart of the defence were Germany and the UK both countries with strong but ageing air forces. Together with Italy they decided to develop a new aircraft, initially known as the Multi Role Combat Aircraft which, if nothing else, reflects the fact that none of the countries wanted the same thing from their aircraft. Huge experience in the partnership came from

BAC, now BAe Systems, in the UK, MBB, now EADS, in Germany and Aeritalia, now Alenia, in Italy. At the beginning the Netherlands were also partners but they pulled out in 1970 citing that the development would be too complicated.

Panavia was the new company formed to build the aircraft and was jointly owned by the three countries. It might be thought that what evolved could be the worst of all worlds but perhaps the opposite was actually true. The Tornado, as it became known, proved to be a stable and rugged combat aircraft that lived up to its original multi role requirements.

Some big names of aviation were involved in the Tornado's creation. Director of Flight Operations was Roland Beamont, famous as a wartime fighter

ABOVE

A Panavia Tornado GR1
from 16 Squadron RAF
on patrol over Germany
during the final days of
the Cold War

pilot and test pilot for the Canberra and Lightning. Marketing the aircraft was ex Spitfire test pilot and Battle of Britain fighter pilot Jeffrey Quill.

The aircraft that finally flew in 1974 was true to its word. The Tornado GR1 was bought by all three partners and subsequently by Saudi Arabia as well. Effectively this was a bomber designed to replace the Vulcan and Buccaneer in RAF service, the Lockheed Starfighter in both the Luftwaffe and the then West German Navy as well as the Italian Air Force. All had slightly different roles and used a variety of weapons. A further variant, the ADV or F.3 was also bought by the RAF as a true air defence fighter.

So it seemed that that the concerns of various countries wanting different roles from the same aircraft were misplaced. Orders were placed for almost 1,000 aircraft, deliveries were almost on time and squadrons began to form on the aircraft in the early 1980s. It was, however, to be almost ten years before the Tornado had a chance to prove itself in combat. The Gulf War of 1991 was a real test. Hot, dusty and humid conditions made operations difficult enough let alone the Iraqi air defences and while actual results are hard to quantify it has been claimed that the bombing of airfields, munitions depots and other Iraqi targets was some of the most accurate in the history of the RAF. Six aircraft were shot down and the world saw the TV images of Tornado crew after capture in Iraq. However the Tornado GR1 did its job and has carried on doing so. A mid-life upgrade to GR4 standard and further deployments to Kosovo, Libya, and Iraq again in 2003 have meant that this fine aircraft has proved itself again and again and it looks as though it will stay in RAF service until 2019.

Design & Artwork: ALEX YOUNG

Published by: DEMAND MEDIA LIMITED

Publisher: JASON FENWICK

Written by: COLIN HIGGS